VELOCITY

OVERDRIVE

THE ROAD TO REINVENTION

Dale Pollak

New Year Publishing LLC
Danville, California

Velocity Overdrive

by Dale Pollak

© 2013 by New Year Publishing, LLC
144 Diablo Ranch Ct.
Danville, CA 94506 USA
http://www.newyearpublishing.com

ISBN 9781935547389
Library of Congress Control Number:

CONTENTS

ACKNOWLEDGEMENTS

I am deeply grateful and indebted to all of the dealers and industry experts who shared their time, insights and guidance for this book. Their contributions were both inspiring and instrumental in helping me achieve the goal of publishing a third book that helps the broader dealer community improve their businesses and satisfy the ever-evolving needs of today's customers.

I would also like to thank Lance Helgeson for serving as my eyes, ears and sounding board. He's been a trusted backstop for all three of my books. His knack for distilling, organizing and presenting the complexity of velocity management principles ensures a meaningful and motivational read for dealers.

Like its predecessors, *Velocity Overdrive* would not have come to fruition without the tireless effort and energy the entire vAuto team brings to their jobs every day. Their commitment and loyalty to our dealer customers and mission affords me the opportunity to contemplate, undertake and complete another book-writing project. In particular, I would like to thank my hard-working and ever-bright assistant, Susan Taft. Without her, I would never be able to balance the work on this book with the day-to-day demands our business requires.

I also owe a heart-felt thanks to Chip Perry and the entire AutoTrader Group organization. It's rare for an entrepreneur to be truly happy after selling a business to a larger partner. Yet, here I am exhilarated, inspired and more motivated than ever. It's a thrill to work every day with talented people who share my strong concern for dealers and passionate desire to help them. The energy and enthusiasm I see at all levels of the ATG organization helped fuel the many late nights and weekends spent working on this book.

My family merits an extra-special thank you. This book would not be possible without the dedication, guidance, patience, support and love my wife, Nancy, gives me every day. In addition, I'm eternally grateful for the greatest gift we share, our sons Austin, Alex and Samson. Their fresh insights, cut-to-the-quick humor and can-do attitudes are a constant and fulfilling reminder that our blessings grow the more we give.

Finally, I would like to thank you, the reader. I'm extremely fortunate to count many of you as friends. I consider your confidence and trust in me, and this book, as one of my most profound blessings.

PREFACE
A THANK-YOU TO SAMSON
AND SPONGEBOB SQUAREPANTS

Last summer, I was enjoying a late afternoon beer at our family's lakeside vacation home in Michigan, thinking about the car business.

My 13-year-old son, Samson, had just finished the day's last ride on a Waverunner, and came off the dock dripping wet.

"What are you thinking about?" he asked, grabbing a towel.

"I'm thinking about the car business and another book," I said.

"What would you write about?" he asked.

I explained how, since my second book, *Velocity 2.0: Paint, Pixels and Profitability*, had been published in early 2010, many dealers were struggling. They were paying a lot more attention to used vehicles, but felt the extra energy, effort and investment wasn't paying off.

"What do you mean?" he asked.

I smiled. This kid definitely has his old man's curiosity and penchant for persistent questions.

I explained the difficulties confronting dealers—the ongoing compression of transaction profit margins due to increased competition and the Internet, harder-to-find used vehicle supplies and the inevitable struggle that arises as dealers feel forced to adapt to a more challenging business environment that requires greater efficiencies to succeed. On top of that, I noted, dealers were seeing signs of life in new vehicles—which raised the prospect that many might simply abandon their necessity-driven interest in used vehicles altogether.

"My concern is for the dealers who don't step in and step up," I told Samson. "The best I can tell, the dealers who become the most efficient in everything they do will find the profits and prosperity they seek. Those who don't embrace this evolution will get left behind."

Samson was silent for a moment, letting what I'd said sink in.

"Sounds like dealers need to shift into overdrive, like SpongeBob Squarepants driving to get to a Krabby Patty," Samson said.

God bless this kid, I thought. He absolutely nailed it. Shift into Overdrive. That's exactly what dealers need to do.

"Thank you, Samson," I said.

"For what?" he asked.

"You just gave me the title for my next book, *Velocity Overdrive*," I said.

He smiled. I finished my beer and took his hand. "C'mon, son. Let's go see what's cooking for dinner."

Introduction:
The Road to Reinvention

It's been a challenging ride for every franchised car dealer the past four years. The economy tanked. Sales dried up. Profits dwindled.

But the strongest have survived. That's you, the dealer reading this book.

You're here because, somewhere along the way, you made a choice about your used vehicle department. You've decided the time has come to give it more attention and get a better return on your investment for this side of your business.

Good for you. It was, and still is, a smart choice.

If nothing else, the economic downturn proved that a dealer's used vehicle department is a lifeline for survival. Unlike new vehicle departments, which are inextricably tied to factory production schedules and vehicle allocations, the used vehicle department is under the dealer's sole control and discretion. It's the one place where you, the dealer, set the pace for sales volumes and profitability.

As dealers shifted their focus to used vehicles, some made huge gains. They adopted velocity principles and began achieving impressive increases in sales and profits. You might say they're doing gang-busters in this side of the business.

This book is about these dealers and their stories. It's about the road to reinvention these dealers undertook as they set their sights on more market share and improved profitability. It's about the inef-ficiencies they encountered in people and processes as they adopted velocity management principles and ran headlong into trouble.

I've been lucky to have had a front-row seat to what is a truly remarkable transformation in the way some dealers now think about and manage their used vehicle departments. Metrics and data are the name of the game today for buying/pricing cars, managing inventory, making appraisals, recon-ditioning cars, desking deals and, perhaps most important, guiding people and their performance.

Of course, I'd like to think I've had a little something to do with this shift to a metrics- and market-driven mindset for managing used vehicle departments. I'm the guy that introduced the Velocity Method of Management™ to car dealers through my previous books, *Velocity: From the Front Line to the Bottom Line* and *Velocity 2.0: Paint, Pixels & Profitability.* I'm also the guy who founded a technology company that allows dealers to access these metrics and market data and use them to guide a new way of doing business.

I would like to say everything is hunky-dory in the land of velocity management.

But it isn't. That's why I've been talking to dealers who've embarked on the road to reinvention. It's the reason I'm writing this book.

You see, the economic downturn hastened what is known as a "race to efficiencies" in the car business. This race isn't just about being leaner and meaner, and doing more with less. That's pretty much a given in any retail business these days.

No, this is a race to change the people and pro-cesses in a dealership, starting in used vehicles, to make everything run in a more efficient manner to yield a better return on investment and greater profitability.

A lot of dealers are struggling with this road to reinvention. As I've studied their difficulties, I've come to understand the problems are largely due to a lack of fortitude or understanding about what it means to embark on a road to reinvention in a truly dealership-holistic manner.

This road is not yet a well-paved or well-marked pathway to profits and prosperity. There are, however, some dealers who have ventured farther, and seen more success, than others.

For these dealers, the road to reinvention and greater operational efficiencies is now a way of life. In most cases, these dealers have no desire to turn back or change course. They've got a new lease on life for their businesses and their future fortunes.

The degree and scope of change and innovation these velocity-focused dealers have embraced to achieve a greater level of operational efficiencies is sometimes breath-taking. They really are reinventing and retooling their dealerships for the rest of the 21st Century.

My goal for this book is to highlight the road to reinvention, potholes and all, these dealers have traveled as they adopted velocity management in used vehicles and made "turn and earn" a strategic, efficiency-focused imperative in every dealership department.

I'm grateful these dealers openly talked about their difficulties and lessons learned. In addition to insights that help other dealers become more efficient and profitable, they share inspiration. If I might say so, it's pretty cool stuff!

We have a lot of ground to cover in the subsequent pages. The attempt here is to reflect as much of the rationale for and details of this holistic, efficiency-driven road to reinvention these dealers have undertaken.

For this reason, I'll only spend a brief time reviewing velocity metrics and principles addressed in my earlier books, and do so mostly to highlight how technology and fresh data have made this an even more efficient, precise and profitable way to manage used vehicle operations.

With that, I'd like to thank you for choosing this book and welcome you to the road to reinvention.

Enjoy the read.

A Road to Reinvention Pioneer

Russ Wallace was a natural in the used car business.

The former director of used vehicle operations at the Bill Marsh Group, Traverse City, Mich., was an early and eager adopter of the Velocity Method of Management™. Wallace loved how velocity metrics measured the supply and demand of specific vehicles, helped him pinpoint market hot spots and pitfalls, and enabled him to quickly adjust his inventory to anticipate these inherent swings.

Wallace had an indelible eye for spotting inefficiencies in his used vehicle operations. He had a special zest for reinvention when it would result in a better way of doing things.

With Wallace's help, the Marsh group was one of the first dealers to recognize that centralizing the sourcing, reconditioning and detailing of vehicles would reduce the costs and time required to acquire a vehicle, get it front-line ready and post it online for potential buyers.

"Russ said, 'let's run this like a separate business,'" recalls dealer Mike Marsh, son of the five-store group founder, Bill Marsh, Sr. "We centralized everything—acquiring the cars, transporting the cars, reconditioning, putting them online and getting them on the lot when needed.

"We completely separated the function of the sales manager from having anything to do with inventory management," Marsh says. "Russ went to our service director and body shop and said, 'this is stupid that we're fighting each other. Let's figure this out.' We became extremely efficient."

Wallace also spotted and addressed other inefficiencies. He recognized that age kills used vehicle gross profit potential. He was a stickler for getting rid of cars that hit the 30-day mark. When they did, they were gone, with any incurred wholesale loss charged to the respective dealership's used vehicle department.

This strict policy meant, of course, that Wallace had occasional tussles with sales managers who questioned why he was getting rid of a perfectly good used vehicle. His typical response: "Why didn't you sell it?"

Such confrontations are part of the day-to-day balancing act between the velocity-focused needs of the dealership to "turn and earn" inventory to maximize each vehicle's return on investment (ROI), and a sales manager's desire to have more vehicles to make more deals. In sales, a bigger selection traditionally means more opportunities to land a customer on a car.

Wallace understood this and mitigated the tension with a unique "raw material" approach to inventory management. He'd use velocity metrics and market data to forecast inventory needs for each of Marsh's five dealerships. He'd then place vehicles from auctions and trade-ins into his "raw material," and use these vehicles to quickly replace those that sold and didn't.

This reinvention of inventory management meant sales managers couldn't really complain. Wallace would make sure they had their full complement of inventory filled at all times, with vehicles that velocity metrics and market data indicated would be good, profit-generating sellers.

Before the advent of technology and tools that provided the velocity metrics and market data on individual vehicles, Wallace tracked every vehicle's age, status ("raw material," in transit, in process, on the lot), price adjustments and other characteristics on dry-erase boards in his office. His goal: Turn Marsh's 300-unit inventory 15-16 times per year, which required balancing each unit's time in raw material (about 10 days) and on the lot (about 20 days).

He used a team approach to determine average reconditioning costs, meeting with sales managers, appraisers and managers at Marsh's reconditioning/sourcing center. He tracked all those numbers, too, to ensure estimates were on the money and each vehicle hit the lot with maximum profit potential.

When I visited Wallace's office, I got the sense I was in the presence of a brilliant professor, a guy with complex equations on a chalkboard, a bright eye, a smile and a kid-like excitement to point out his latest insight or process change.

"Russ was very disciplined and looked at the business strategically," Mike Marsh says. "He didn't view it deal by deal, or car by car. Each was part of a larger picture. He had a vision for how we could operate more efficiently and he understood technology."

In other words, Wallace was a rare bird among used vehicle managers—a savvy strategist who understood how velocity management principles and efficiencies can work hand-in-hand to spur reinvention.

In fact, Wallace's insights have helped me reinvent and recalibrate velocity management metrics and principles to make the job of managing used vehicle inventory easier for dealers.

He taught me an important lesson: It's virtually impossible to manage used vehicle inventory on the basis of specific makes and models. To be sure, you need to know the makes/models/equipment and trim packages that sell quickest. However, from a strategic management perspective, it's better to think of the shape and type of vehicles and their price points to drive the acquisition of specific units.

This, as Wallace would often say, is a more efficient way to ensure inventory management decisions reflect how used vehicle buyers actually shop for cars—they think first of a type of vehicle and price they can afford, and then look for vehicles that fit these parameters. It makes perfect sense for dealers to align their inventory decisions to meet these buyer dynamics.

Wallace's profound insight led to the development of velocity-driven technology and tools that dealers can now use to adopt the same strategic and efficiency-focused approach to inventory management that he pioneered. In the next chapter, we'll begin discussing the evolution of velocity metrics and management principles to what I now call "provisioning" inventory.

I've chosen to start this book by focusing a bit on my good friend Russ Wallace for three reasons:

1. **It's cathartic.** I'm still coming to terms with Russ's untimely death last summer. He died in his son's arms after a tragic weekend accident while they were out riding dirt bikes on his birthday. I miss Russ. I miss his laugh, his zest for life, his interest in reinvention and his unique approach to the used vehicle business. He was a gem of a man with a beautiful, efficiency-focused, business-smart mind.

2. **His success is exemplary.** Russ didn't arrive at his insights on velocity-driven efficiencies and reinvention overnight. He spent a lot of time and effort realigning the people and processes at the Marsh group to bring his vision for a better, more efficient way of managing used vehicles to life. As other dealers head down the velocity-paved road to reinvention and efficiencies, they will inevitably run into critical decisions and management challenges. As this occurs, dealers would do well to remember one of Russ's favorite sayings, "Life isn't fair, and it ain't easy. Get on with it."

3. **Sharing is caring.** Russ spent countless hours offering insights from his own road to efficiencies and reinvention with other velocity-minded

dealers. They would travel from all around
the country to understand the way he thought
about and approached the business. Russ wasn't
afraid to poke a little to make a point—much
like he stood his ground with sales managers.
"Wouldn't you be better off if...?" was a typical
lead-in Russ would offer as dealers shared their
struggles to implement velocity principles and
achieve greater efficiencies. It is my hope that
Russ's generous spirit and willingness to share
lives on in this book.

A Review of Inventory Vital Signs

Don't let the mint condition, red and white '57 Corvette in Bill Stasek's showroom fool you.

This guy is anything but an "old school car dealer," especially when it comes to used vehicles.

"We were the traditional dealer who would acquire the car, put it out there and let it sit for 30 days," Stasek says. "If it didn't sell, maybe you'd drop the price and wait another 30 days.

"Then it gets to 60 days and you put a spiff on it to motivate the sales people to sell it. Then you drop the price again and by the time you're done, you're losing money on the car and you're paying big money to the salespeople. It's a foolish, foolish way to do business."

I'm seated in Stasek's wood-paneled conference room on a Tuesday morning, Valentine's Day, and we're reviewing 16 vehicles in Stasek's 80-car inventory that have reached 46 or more days old. We're joined by dealership general manager and Stasek's brother, Bob Stasek, and the store's assistant used vehicle manager, Jorge Soto.

Soto's laptop is connected to a big screen, which displays each vehicle's listing in the store's inventory management system. We're examining each car's "back story," or the reasons each vehicle has yet to attract buyers.

We're focused, for the moment, on a loaded, gray 2008 Chevrolet Equinox with 86,000 miles. It's an outlier at 130 days—an anomaly Stasek attributes to easing the store's 60-days-and-it's-gone policy during winter months.

"The market day's supply (120 days) is very high, but this is a car that sells well for us and this one is loaded," Stasek says. "We're number one in price (95 percent price to market) and right in the hunt with condition and miles."

"I look at the car and it should've sold," adds Bob Stasek.

He points to Soto's notes about pricing and other adjustments made to the vehicle's online listings to get more buyer attention during its time in inventory: "Horrible clicks. Moved price slightly. Very little action. Moved under $11,000. Few clicks. Dropped price. Featured AWD in description."

"It's not like we haven't been on it," Bob Stasek says.

He sums up the group's conclusion on the vehicle: "We should have looked at that in 45 days and said, 'Okay, Dummies. Let's get rid of this car.'"

I share this exchange because it is a good example of the bumps and learning curves velocity-oriented dealers encounter as they travel the road to reinvention and greater efficiencies in their used vehicle operations. Even though dealers like Stasek are now armed with market-focused data and management metrics, the way they interpret those metrics, and the decisions that follow, can sometimes lead to an aging problem.

"Yes, we're struggling with old inventory. But that's not going to change my opinion of velocity management," Stasek says. "This is our fault and our judgment that's at fault. These cars started their life as used cars at a time when we weren't getting a lot of traffic. We should have gotten rid of some of these cars before they became a problem."

Stasek's faith in velocity management isn't misplaced. He and his team have been dutiful stewards of velocity management metrics and principles for nearly the past two years. The attention and vigilance they've paid to their used vehicle inventory has resulted in a more than doubling of monthly sales from 35 to 80 units.

In many ways, the conference room review of Stasek's aging vehicles resembles a group of physicians reviewing a patient's chart to see why his condition has not improved. Just like the medical professionals, who would likely review blood pressure, breathing and other vital signs to orient their thinking and potential prescriptive measures, Stasek and other velocity dealers focus on the four baseline vital signs for their inventory and specific vehicles to assess each car's standing and determine next steps.

VITAL SIGN 1: MARKET DAYS SUPPLY

This metric measures the supply and demand characteristics of each vehicle in a dealer's specific market. It shows the number of the same or similar vehicles available in a dealer's market area, as well as the number that have sold in the past 45 days. Example: If there are 10 vehicles available in a market, and the sales rate is 1 per day over 45 days, the vehicle's market days supply is 10 (see figure, next page).

Velocity dealers like Stasek who track this metric understand it offers a sense of the ease or difficulty they'll have selling a vehicle. Take the 2008 Equinox: Its market days supply of 120 days suggests the unit's got a fair amount of competition, which

> **Market Days Supply**
> 10 Vehicles ÷ 1 per day over 45 days
> equals
> 10 Days Supply

means its price point must be competitive to attract customers.

Soto understands this and has positioned the vehicle's price to be a market-leader compared to similar available units. "Market days supply gives you the ability to understand what it takes to move a vehicle," he says. "If the number's lower, it sells faster; if it's higher, you've got to make the vehicle stand out."

Soto is correct. In general, the history of velocity dealers suggests that vehicles with a market days supply metric of 65 days or less are the top performers. This figure, for some dealers, becomes their overall target for the average market days supply for their entire inventory.

There are two, logical reasons for this:

1. **There are fewer of these vehicles available.** This means dealers who acquire these cars have a distinct advantage. Buyers who want these vehicles know they are harder to find and, as a result, are likely to spend more time and energy looking for them. For dealers, this translates to less expense and energy positioning these vehicles for

maximum online attention in the early stages of their lifecycle. To borrow a concept from *Field of Dreams*, once you build and ready these vehicles for retail, the buyers will typically come.

2. **There's less price competition for these vehicles.** This stands to reason given there are fewer of them available to buyers. Dealers still need to offer competitive price points, but the supply and demand dynamics of vehicles with lower market days supply metrics provide a natural insulation against market price sensitivity.

For most dealers, the dynamics around market days supply should be keenly familiar. The reference point? Your new vehicle department, where hot new models result in buyers at your door and MSRP-and-above pricing that rarely gets push-back from buyers because of the scarcity of the vehicles and their desire to own one.

But, as we all know, we can't thrive as car dealers by focusing solely on the hottest new or used vehicles. This approach can yield short-term benefits but it's not a sustainable strategy for the long haul, where the goal is to consistently build sales volumes and gross profits. As a result, velocity dealers will use the market days supply metric to guide the overall composition of their inventory, offering a mix of high-, mid- and lower-level market days supply vehicles to maximize their inventory's appeal to the broadest range of buyers.

VITAL SIGN 2: COST TO MARKET

Cost to Market Metric

This metric helps velocity dealers ensure they own their used vehicles "right" from the time they acquire a unit at auction or trade-in until the time they sell the car.

If you own a vehicle for $8,500 and the average retail asking price is $10,000, your Cost to Market metric for this car is 85%. Your "spread" is $1,500.

In essence, the cost to market metric helps dealers manage each used vehicle from an investment perspective. It constantly measures each vehicle's ability to achieve a dealer's goals for gross profit or return on investment (ROI). It does this by measuring the costs associated with each vehicle against its likely retail selling price. The difference between these two numbers, known as the "spread," determines each vehicle's profit potential.

Among the key velocity vital signs, the cost to market metric is often the most difficult for dealers to manage effectively. This is because they are not accustomed to actively and efficiently managing each used vehicle's "spread" in a manner that is in sync with today's used vehicle marketplace.

In the past, dealers controlled the "spread" with little or no regard for the prevailing retail market. They would pay $X for a vehicle at auction or trade, charge the car for reconditioning and a pack, and apply a standard $3,000 to $4,000 mark-up.

Before the Internet, it didn't matter if this traditional approach to managing the "spread" resulted in vehicles priced above the same or similar competing vehicles. Customers had to work hard, and visit a lot of dealerships, to truly know if a dealer's price was "the best in town." This also meant dealers didn't need to pay super-close attention to the costs they incurred for, or charged to, each vehicle.

Today, however, the Internet has changed these dynamics. Used vehicle buyers are instantly aware of a bad price and won't give that car a second look. This marketplace efficiency has put the squeeze on a dealer's "spread" or margin for a return on investment (ROI)—in effect, the ceiling of the "spread" is coming down.

At the same time, the floor of the "spread" has, in recent years, been going up. Industry stats show the average wholesale price of vehicles at auctions has been on a near-steady upward track for the past few years, hovering near $10,000 in spring 2012.

In business jargon, this is known as margin compression—when the floor rises and the ceiling falls for retailers. In most industries, this spurs retail business owners to increase efficiencies and to cut costs.

But many dealers have yet to embrace this new reality. They still expect to see average gross profits, or their ROI in used vehicles, to compare favorably to what they achieved in the past. Even worse, they expect to see this type of return despite little effort to actively increase efficiencies and cut costs.

In subsequent chapters, we'll show how velocity dealers have become better managers of the "spread" as they acquire, recondition, pack and retail used vehicles.

In the meantime, let's simply recognize that controlling costs and increasing efficiencies are essential to maximizing the "spread" on used vehicles, and the cost to market metric is the single-best barometer to achieve these goals.

Here's how the cost to market metric works:

If a dealer acquires a vehicle for $8,500 and the prevailing retail price for the same or similar unit is $10,000, the vehicle's cost to market ratio is 85 percent. This means the dealer has a $1,500 "spread" (15 percent) to cover any acquisition/ transportation fees, the costs to recondition the vehicle and the unit's gross profit potential.

In this example, if a dealer acquired a unit on trade-in for $8,500, and learned it would require $1,200 in reconditioning costs, the best next step would probably be to wholesale the vehicle right away. The reason: The $300 in potential gross profit is not a suitable ROI for the time, energy and costs required to recondition the vehicle and post it online as a retail unit.

This decision, however, is a subjective call each dealer needs to make, depending on their circumstances and the specific retailing prospects for the vehicle. If the car had a low market days supply, for example, it might make sense to retail it, given it's likely to sell quickly and poses less risk of becoming an aging problem.

If a manager like Soto makes this decision, the next step would be to find ways to control reconditioning and pack-related costs and, possibly, look for accessories and other ways to increase its front-end profit potential and overall "spread."

This is the kind of thing retailers like CarMax do for every used vehicle they sell. The company's 2012 fiscal year report boasts the second consecutive year of an average $250 decrease in reconditioning costs across the 408,000 used vehicles the company sold at its stores. Such efforts to control costs reflect a keen understanding of the cost to market metric and the need to manage the "spread" in a highly competitive and margin-compressed retail environment.

Among velocity dealers who have embarked on the road to reinvention and taken significant steps to increase efficiencies and cut costs, the total cost to market average for their inventories is 84 percent. This means these dealers have, on average, a 16 percent "spread" between their acquisition, reconditioning and pack costs for vehicles and the average retail prices for used vehicles in their markets to achieve their gross profit goals in a timely manner.

At Kelley Auto Group, Fort Wayne, Ind., the six-store dealer group's centralized used vehicle sourcing center previously targeted a 78 percent cost to market for inventory acquisitions, says Trent Waybright, director of used vehicle operations.

That parameter proved too tight as wholesale prices have heated up and the stores are aiming to keep more trade-ins. "We're currently targeting 80 percent to 82 percent cost to market," Waybright says. "In the past year, I've allowed that to go up a shade."

Vital Sign 3: Price to Market

This metric measures how the price of a vehicle compares to the average price of the same or similarly equipped competing vehicles in a dealer's market.

As we were evaluating the 2008 Equinox in Bill Stasek's inventory, the price to market metric captured Stasek's attention. He zeroed in on it immediately to see if the unit's competitive price position was a factor behind the vehicle's age. Nope. The vehicle's price positioned it at No. 1 in the market among competing vehicles, a 95 percent price to market.

Price to Market By Vehicle Age

0-15 days	96%
15-30 days	93%
30-45 days	89%
> 45 days	n/a*

* Assumes 45-day turn policy

For Stasek and other velocity dealers, the price to market metric is as important to them as a patient's heart rate or blood pressure would be to a physician.

The reason? Today's buyers have a far easier time comparing prices for the same or similar cars available in a market. As noted earlier, if a vehicle is priced too high compared to other units online buyers perceive as the same or similar, the chances are pretty good their interest in the vehicle will be limited.

As a result of this market price awareness and sensitivity, many velocity dealers have created a strategy for how they position their vehicles by price in their markets—typically following the time-tested logic that fresh cars are best able to hold their gross profit potential and stand taller against competing units (see box, this page for a breakdown). Their pricing strategy seeks to balance the need to maintain the velocity of their inventory turn, and maximize each unit's gross profit potential.

The reality of pricing in today's Internet-driven market can be difficult for more traditional dealers to embrace. They still cling to the practice of placing a standard $3,000 to $4,000 mark-up on every vehicle. In this way, dealers often viewed pricing as a means to achieve their gross profit per unit goals. In today's environment, this "old school" way of thinking can be a death knell for a vehicle's profit prospects.

"Price is a way to build traffic," affirms Jack Anderson, used vehicle director at West Herr Automotive, Buffalo, N.Y. "Your profit comes from everything else you do, the efficiencies of the processes around each retail vehicle."

Thank you, Jack. I couldn't have said it better myself. We'll examine these efficiency- and profit-focused processes in upcoming chapters.

In the meantime, it's worth addressing another misconception many tradition-focused dealers hold about pricing used vehicles in today's retail environment: Attuning your vehicle prices to your market does not necessarily mean you need to be the lowest-priced provider.

"Look at CarMax," says dealer Bill Pearson, formerly of Finish Line Ford, Peoria, Ill. "They're never the cheapest in any market. They're not negotiating and they're selling a ton of cars. Nobody said you've got to be the cheapest to be the best."

Indeed, velocity dealers who are further down the road to reinvention have also realized that competitive prices and processes, combined with the right cars, can make customers look past a price differential of several hundred dollars.

Stasek sees this competitive pricing dynamic getting ever sharper.

"More and more dealers are on some kind of used car pricing tool," he says. "The dealers who don't do this are either going to be gone or they're going to be small-town dealers that strictly sell to their local population, and possibly don't need these tools. A lot of dealers are in this game now and they're not sitting still. They're watching their cars the same way we're watching ours."

VITAL SIGN 4: AVERAGE AGE OF INVENTORY

As noted above, the freshest used cars stand tallest, in terms of pricing and potential profit, for dealers.

This should come as no surprise to even the most traditional dealers when they ask this question: Of all the cars in the used vehicle inventory, which ones are likely to generate the most excitement among salespeople? The answer, invariably, are the vehicles that just hit the lot.

The same dynamic is true for today's buyers. As they search online for vehicles that fit their needs and price points, they'll likely pay the greatest

attention to units they haven't seen before, provided these cars match their purchase preferences.
(A quick online merchandising tip: This is why it
pays to shuffle photos and change descriptions
on aging units, creating a sheen of freshness, even
though they may be long in tooth.)

Dealers like Stasek who are traveling the road
to reinvention in their used vehicle departments
recognize this dynamic. In fact, it's the key reason
we're sitting in his conference room to discuss aged
vehicles. These cars, after all, are a drag on the
overall desirability of his inventory, not to mention
his goals for profitability and ROI.

Stasek likes to maintain an average age of inventory near 30 days to achieve his goal of turning his
80-car inventory 12 times a year. Other velocity
dealers are more aggressive, aiming for an average
inventory age between 20 and 25 days to turn their
inventories 15 to 18 times a year.

These inventory age and turn parameters can be
difficult for traditional dealers to recognize as
important. The National Automobile Dealers Association pegs the average inventory turn rate at six
times a year for franchised dealers. This translates
to inventory age policies that allow vehicles to age
60 days and longer.

In my view, these inventory age and turn
benchmarks are out of step with today's highly
competitive, more volatile and margin-compressed

used vehicle environment. I believe this for two reasons:

First, used vehicle depreciation still exists. The longer a used vehicle remains on a dealer's lot, the more depreciation will corrode a dealer's ability to maximize the car's ROI potential. Dealers have long intuited this dynamic, making price adjustments to sell aging vehicles more quickly and reduce the effects of depreciation. This is why, as the chart on this page shows, the gross profit potential diminishes as the age and carrying costs of a vehicle increase.

Some dealers may incorrectly view rising wholesale prices as a reason to say "it's okay to let vehicles age because I can't replace this unit for what I

How Vehicle Age Affects Profit Potential

Age	Cost to Market*	Mark-up**
0-15	84 percent	$2,100
15-30	86 percent	$1,800
30-45	88 percent	$1,600
> 45	90 percent	$1,400

* Cost to Market measures the ratio between a vehicle's total cost (e.g., acquisition/reconditioning costs and pack) and average retail price point for the vehicle.

** Mark-up is the amount dealers add to their total vehicle costs to achieve the gross profit margin.

paid." This view fails to recognize the ongoing costs to maintain the unit's retail-readiness, and the lost opportunity to sell the vehicle and redeploy the investment in a fresh car that will sell more quickly.

Second, the traditional inventory age and turn benchmarks do not reflect the full investment potential in used vehicles dealers could enjoy if they got more aggressive with velocity's turn-and-earn inventory management principles.

Think of it this way: These benchmarks are effectively saying, if I invest $1 million in my inventory, it's okay to turn this investment six times a year and accept my depreciation-driven wholesale losses. Meanwhile, a growing number of dealers aim for turning their inventory investment 12 to 18 times a year to maximize their ROI and, in effect, create "found" money in service, parts, detailing and F&I departments.

For dealers who are in the initial stages of velocity management and the road to reinvention, I recommend they maintain at least 50 percent of their inventory below 30 days of age.

By design, this benchmark effectively focuses efforts to manage all inventory vital signs in tandem with each other—knowing the market days supply of vehicles you acquire, paying the "right" price to allow sufficient "spread," and pricing them "right" to move quickly.

Vital Signs + Reinvention = Success

Most of us recognize that vital signs alone do not guarantee a long, healthy and productive life. It takes discipline and effort, especially as we age, to make exercise, eating right and getting sufficient rest (all the things our doctors tell us to do) part of our daily routine to maintain a healthy set of vital signs.

Even then, however, we have no guarantee of longevity. We've all heard the stories of someone in "perfect health" who suddenly passes away.

That said, however, it's far more likely that we'll live a healthy life if we actively take the time and make the effort to maintain our vital signs and individual health.

The same is true for used vehicle inventories. Dealers who are diligent stewards of these velocity-based vital signs are better able to maximize their returns on investment and minimize depreciation and wholesale losses in their used vehicle departments. They are in the best position for long-term success and prosperity.

But such end results do not come easy or without pain (much like the muscle soreness we endure as we strive for fitness). As we'll see in upcoming chapters, these vital signs often expose inefficiencies in people and processes in used vehicle and other dealership departments. These inefficiencies, and the reinvention required to address them, represent both the pain and gain dealers encounter on the velocity-driven journey to improve used vehicle sales and profitability.

There is good news on this front for dealers: New data, technology and tools are now available to make the job of monitoring and managing used vehicle metrics, and embarking on the road to reinvention and efficiency, easier than it has ever been.

A PARTNERSHIP FOR PROGRESS

Not long after I published my second book, I started getting phone calls from suitors for my company.

To a person, these callers were impressed with vAuto's efforts to pioneer the velocity style of used vehicle management in the retail automotive industry. They liked how we'd provided both technology and tools to affect a significant change in the way dealers managed their used vehicle operations to meet the needs of an Internet-driven retail environment.

These callers also liked vAuto's unique approach with its customers, providing one-on-one coaches to help dealers understand and master velocity management principles and metrics in their used vehicle operations. They regarded our performance managers as a sign of the company's commitment to help dealers embrace a new way of doing business and achieving success.

I was flattered by the praise. What entrepreneur wouldn't be? These callers were affirming that my vision for velocity management and vAuto had fully and finally arrived.

But once these conversations got past the praise, they almost always fell short. This occurred after I asked a very direct and simple question: How would a joint venture with your company help dealers become more efficient and successful?

The answers I got were unsatisfying and, in some cases, even a bit insulting. Too often, these callers really didn't care much for the success of dealers. To them, dealers were dollar signs. They viewed a joint venture or buy-out of vAuto as simply a way to increase their industry position and make even more money.

My question was also self-serving. I'd already begun work to refine the technology and tools that power velocity metrics and management principles. I had recognized that the adoption of velocity management spurred a road to reinvention for dealers. My question was really a test to see if any of these potential suitors had their eyes on this horizon and understood its implications.

Then I got a call from Chip Perry, CEO at Auto-Trader.com. I've known Chip over the years and respected his leadership and vision. He's built AutoTrader.com into the nation's leading classified automotive marketplace, making it one of the few dotcoms to emerge from the '90s with a viable and successful business plan.

I asked the same question of Perry that I put to the other callers. This time, the answer I got surprised me.

"To be honest, Dale, we're not really sure. We do know, however, that used vehicles are critically important to dealers and our company. Further, it's imperative that we leverage our family of companies' data and technology to give more value to dealers. That's job one," Perry says. "Could you come to Atlanta and talk about it?"

This is exactly what I wanted to hear. Perry was talking possibilities, not simply profits.

I mulled the prospect of an AutoTrader.com partnership and what it might mean for the evolution of velocity management and dealer success.

For starters, I recognized that AutoTrader.com has become arguably one of the most important partners for dealers who want to sell more vehicles. I spent a fair amount of space in my second book, and countless hours in subsequent discussions with dealers, about the importance of "pixel proficiency" to attract online buyers to vehicles listed on sites like AutoTrader.com and Cars.com.

I also recognized that AutoTrader.com is like a giant voting machine for used vehicle buyers. Every day, they vote on cars with their search strings and mouse-clicks. These "votes" determine the winners among the thousands of available vehicles, and they pinpoint the makes/models, trim levels, equipment configurations and pricing that resonates best with buyers.

It would be extremely cool, and highly beneficial to dealers, if an alliance with AutoTrader.com would allow the opportunity to tabulate these votes in a manner that would aid the decisions of dealers as they acquire, recondition and retail used vehicles. This real-time market intelligence could supplement the available market days supply data and create a significant value-add for dealers.

Through meetings with dealers and guys like Russ Wallace in Traverse City, I also recognized the value the shared ownership of AutoTrader.com and Manheim might bring to dealers, if only it were leveraged in a way that made the job of acquiring vehicles for dealers easier and more efficient.

I'd heard the same things from dozens of velocity dealers: It's draining, painstaking work to develop vehicle buy lists and then manually scour run lists for auctions nationwide to find the cars needed to fill inventory gaps. This was an inefficient, eight to

12-hour process that occurred at least once a week, sometimes more often.

In other words, this wasn't a sustainable path for most dealers, particularly the mission-critical task of acquiring used vehicle inventory that, in some cases, was critical for a dealer's survival.

I had all this in mind as I flew to meet Perry and other AutoTrader.com executives.

The rest, as they say, is history.

I'm very fortunate. I now have a front row seat to help shape the technology and tools that will help dealers gain efficiencies and become more successful used vehicle retailers. Even better, this new alliance with AutoTrader.com will help dealers along their respective roads to reinvention.

As I headed home after those initial meetings in Atlanta, I was energized. It was time for the game-changing product development and the evolution of velocity management principles and metrics to begin in earnest.

But, before we examine this game-changing evolution, the time has come for a reality check—a time to separate the dealers who are serious about efficiency-focused reinvention from those who may be curious but lack the discipline and will to adapt their businesses to a retail environment where investment intelligence matters just as much, if not more, than instinct.

THE ROAD TO REINVENTION REALITY CHECK

I hope the following isn't overly bold or offensive: Many dealers are not, principally and primarily, in the used car business to make a profit.

I say this as a wake-up call, not a sucker-punch.

This wake-up call is necessary, I believe, because many dealers do not fully recognize how much the business of selling used cars has changed in recent years.

This problem owes a bit to tradition. As dealers, we've long believed our business is "different" than other retailers. For 100-plus years, this has been proven true—dealers could, and did, control market supply and demand dynamics for used vehicles.

This gave dealers the ability to price and sell used vehicles on their terms, unless customers pushed back hard enough.

The Internet has, of course, shifted the balance of power in car deals to consumers. Today's Internet-enabled buyers can easily find and sort available vehicles, and quickly eliminate cars and dealers, that don't fit the "market" that they find online.

In financial terms, this is known as an "efficient market." The investment firm Morgan Stanley defines an efficient market as one that occurs "when the information that investors need to make investment decisions is widely available, thoroughly analyzed and regularly used."[1]

This fundamental shift in the retail environment for used vehicles is proving problematic for many dealers, including some who have embarked on the road to reinvention and greater efficiencies in their used vehicle operations.

The problem? They're still running their used vehicle operations with principles and processes that were designed and came of age before the Internet changed the market. Taken together, these tradition-minded management practices are now hurting these dealers' ability to fully reinvent their used vehicle operations and increase their dealership's overall efficiencies and profitability potential.

---

[1]   http://www.morganstanleyindividual.com/customerservice/dictionary/default.asp?letter=E

The prevalence of these tradition-bound beliefs and practices in our industry has led me to the conclusion that while many dealers *say* they want to make money in used vehicles they don't *act* in a way that allows them to maximize their profitability in today's more efficient marketplace.

Even worse, these are often the dealers who complain the most about how little profit they make in their used vehicle departments.

This wake-up call chapter is intended to change all that.

My goal is to lift the veil for these dealers and pinpoint how some aspects of traditional used vehicle retailing undermine their ability to make money in used vehicles and become what one dealer calls "21st Century Retailers."

In addition, this wake-up call is a required stage-setter for the upcoming chapters. The tradition-based beliefs and practices noted below are clear-cut impediments to traveling the road to reinvention and managing used vehicles as investments.

"A Little Age is Okay." Most dealers would agree that used vehicles, by their nature, depreciate in value. Further, most dealers would agree that the declining value of an asset means it's worth less tomorrow than today.

Even so, many dealers do not apply this thinking to their used vehicle assets. For them, "a little age is okay." This owes to the traditional practice of high mark-ups on used vehicles and the wait for the right buyer willing to pay the price. In addition, it owes to a long-standing practice among dealers to ignore the profit-draining effects of depreciation for as long as possible, rather than confront the reality every day.

This mindset often clouds an objective read on a used vehicle department's performance. If you're not really factoring the costs of depreciation into your assessment of a vehicle's profitability, the assessment itself is flawed. In effect, you're giving yourself credit for a profit that hasn't occurred.

Brian Benstock, vice president and general manager at Paragon Honda, New York City, learned this lesson the hard way. He never factored depreciation into his calculus for used vehicle profitability, until he realized that "a little age is okay" actually hurt his performance and profitability potential.

"I used to be the guy bragging about $5,000 average gross per unit in used cars," Benstock says. "I'd price my cars to maximize front-end gross but the average age of my inventory was 150 days. If I took those cars to auction, I'd lose $200,000 to $300,000. When I subtracted that amount from my gross profits, my average gross was really $1,200 or $1,300. That's the silent loss most dealers carry and don't acknowledge."

These days, Benstock thinks of his used cars like a fish retailer thinks about the daily catch. "How long do you want to keep fresh fish in your inventory if you can't refrigerate it?," Benstock asks. "The answer is a couple days at most. The same is true for cars. We need to stop treating them like they'll last forever. Every day, they're getting less and less desirable."

With the elimination of the "a little age is okay" mentality, Benstock has shifted his focus to turning his inventory more quickly to maximize his ROI and profit on every vehicle. This quick-turn mindset eliminates depreciation and wholesale loss risks and generates sales and profits in other departments.

"The average age of our inventory is less than 30 days. That's really been a game-changer for us," he says. "I won't get into the specifics on the profitability of the dealership but it's never been higher. We're making a bloody fortune."

For other dealers, there's no mistaking Benstock's motivations for being in the used car business. His principal and primary goal is to maximize his profitability and ROI in used vehicles.

A Too-Narrow Focus on Monthly Volumes. Many traditional dealers track the success of their used vehicle departments by evaluating the number of cars they sold in a given month against a running monthly or yearly average.

If the used vehicle department's monthly tally exceeds this benchmark by 20 percent, the dealer is likely to congratulate his managers and salespeople for a job well done.

But what if the overall sales in the dealer's market increased 40 percent or more? In this scenario, the 20 percent increase doesn't seem like such a good job. In fact, it suggests the dealership ceded sales to the competition.

This example illustrates why simply focusing on a store's monthly sales, rather than comparing the tally to the overall market, is a sign of a dealer whose principal and primary focus in used cars isn't maximum profitability.

In today's environment, it's essential to know who's selling what in a given market for dealers to make meaningful comparisons and judgments about their own used vehicle department performance—to essentially know whether a good job is, in fact, worthy of an "atta boy!" for the used vehicle department.

"A good job for us is 23 percent to 27 percent market share, depending on the store," says dealer Mike Marsh of the Bill Marsh Auto Group, Traverse City. "We dominate our market but don't always sell the most cars. For us, market share isn't the only factor. We look at variable net profit, total dealership profit and volume, too."

This is the kind of analysis that profit- and velocity-focused dealers like Marsh undertake as they evaluate the monthly performance of their used vehicle departments. To them, a "good job" in used vehicles must assess what happens in the showroom and beyond to be meaningful.

Too many cars in used vehicle inventories. In the past, it wasn't uncommon for dealers to carry twice the number of vehicles in their inventories than they sold in a given month. For example, if a dealership sold 100 used vehicles a month, the inventory would often run about 200 total cars (a.k.a., a 60-day supply of cars).

In today's marketplace, a 60-day supply is too many vehicles for a dealer whose principal and primary interest is maximizing profitability in used vehicles. Consider the following example:

There are two dealerships side by side in an auto mall, a Ford and a Chevy store. In the past month, the Ford store sold 150 vehicles, the Chevy store sold 60. Most dealers would say the Ford store did a better job, based solely on volume.

But let's say the Ford store had a 60-day supply of vehicles (300 total units for a total investment of $3 million, assuming a $10,000 average cost per unit) and the Chevy store had a 20-day supply of vehicles (40 units for a total investment of $400,000).

Now, let's assume both stores earned a $2,000 front-end gross profit on every car. This means the Ford store made $300,000 from its $3 million investment, a 10 percent return; the Chevy store made $120,000 from its $400,000 investment, a 30 percent return.

Few dealers would disagree that the Chevy store is doing a better job, from an investment perspective, than the Ford store. In addition, the Chevy dealership is turning its inventory roughly three times as fast as the Ford dealership. Given this, it's fair to assume the Chevy store has far less, if any, exposure to inventory depreciation and wholesale losses than the Ford store.

While many dealers understand the profit-positive effects of a fast-turning inventory, it's often a struggle for them to break the habit of stocking a 60-day supply or more of used vehicles. They understand the theory behind the Chevy store's inventory ROI, but they fail to put the principles in practice at their dealerships.

My recommendation: In today's environment, dealers should not carry more than a 45-day supply of vehicles. The market is too volatile and a dealer's cash too important to carry a larger number of cars and expose the investment to depreciation and wholesale losses.

In addition, a 45-day supply is a positive step toward managing used vehicles as an investment that warrants a maximum return. In upcoming chapters, we'll examine how velocity dealers have gone even further, setting aggressive targets of 20-, 25- and 30-day supplies to maximize their profitability in used vehicles.

Packs on Cars[2]: When I was a dealer, I loved packs. They were a way for me to protect my dealership profit in used vehicles, given I couldn't always count on my sales team to "hold gross" and I would invariably have wholesale losses in my inventory.

In those days, we would put a $1,000 pack on every used vehicle we sold. I viewed packs like most dealers: They were a necessary way to hedge profitability and, perhaps more important, we could get away with adding them to every used vehicle.

Times are different now, I'm afraid. In today's efficient and highly competitive used vehicle marketplace, packs are fast becoming a relic of yesterday's retailing best practices. Even worse, they can drag down a dealer's ability to maximize efficiencies and profitability in used vehicle operations.

Put another way, packs are really a tax a dealer imposes on every used vehicle—an add-on that increases the unit's cost but does not enhance the vehicle's overall value.

---

[2] Packs on Cars: A pack is a dealer-determined amount added to the cost of a vehicle. It does not enhance the vehicle's value to the customer. Historically, dealers used packs to offset overhead costs, cover unexpected operating expenses and/or increase the profitability of vehicle sales.

"I don't think you can pack your inventory in today's market the way we used to, be competitive and turn your inventory," says Marc Ray, vice president and partner at Grogan's Towne Chrysler, Toledo. "I used to pack my cars for $1,000 and I've weaned that down to $200. The problem for many dealers is that packs are like crack."

Ray and other dealers on the road to reinvention agree that packs are now problematic in today's environment for three key reasons:

1. **They crimp your profit margin.** Few dealers would argue that the margins in today's used vehicle business are shrinking. There's less room between acquisition costs and retail prices than their used to be to make a profit, and this "spread" is getting smaller.

   For most businesses, such margin compression would sound the alarm bells. They would do everything they could to manage the "spread," and they'd likely focus first and foremost on cutting costs and improving efficiencies.

   But what do dealers do? They add costs to every vehicle in the form of a pack—sometimes to the tune of $1,000. This means dealers are advancing the shrinkage of their "spread" for every car.

   This is why velocity dealers like Ray have limited the amount of cost they add to each used vehicle transaction. They want a clear-eyed and pure read of each vehicle's profit potential and packs typically muddy these waters. They have come to understand their automotive retail business isn't "different" than other retailers.

I frequently hear dealers complain about low front-end gross profits on used vehicles. These same dealers, however, do not recognize how their packs contribute to this problem. This is an illogical position when one considers how packs raise unit costs and reduce profit margin potential.

I'm not suggesting dealers cannot or should not add packs to used vehicles. It's every dealer's prerogative. I do, however, think dealers should be honest with themselves about the relationship between the practice of packing vehicles and their expectations for front-end gross profits on used cars.

2. **Packs make your prices less appealing.** When dealers add the cost of the pack to a used vehicle, they need to raise the unit's price to cover it. In today's efficient market, this is an invitation for today's price-sharp buyers to skip past your used vehicles. The extra $800 to $1,000 many dealers still apply to their vehicles means today's online buyers see a bunch of cars at ABC Motors priced higher than the competition. These vehicles and the dealership probably won't get many second looks, based on price alone.

3. **Packs hurt appraisals.** When I work with dealerships that say they have a hard time finding
vehicles at the "right" price at auctions, I'll take
a closer look at the job they're doing with trade-
ins. I'll examine metrics for each appraiser that
measure their close ratio (e.g., the look to book)
and how close their appraisals meet dealership
targets for the initial margin "spread" for vehicle
acquisitions (e.g., the acquisition cost to market
metric).

The velocity dealers with the best appraisal
performances typically close 40 percent or more
of the appraisals they offer, and they often target
their acquisition cost to market at 80 percent.

When I see a dealership that isn't hitting these
numbers, I'll ask the dealer and managers
whether the store packs cars and, if so, by how
much.

I ask the questions because I've come to recognize a correlation: The size of a dealership pack
varies inversely with its closing ratio on appraisals. That is, the higher the pack, the lower the
close ratios. I've also come to understand that
this dynamic is most profound at dealerships
where packs run north of $500.

Appraisers know, whether dealers want to admit
it or not, that their offers to customers must
account for the dealership's pack. This means
they back off rather than step up. Meanwhile,

customers, who've already used online resources to get a ballpark value for their trade-in, find the appraiser's low-ball number unacceptable.

The end result: Fewer opportunities "at your front door," the most cost-friendly and –effective place to acquire cars.

This dynamic often goes unnoticed by dealers and managers—some of whom complain about their inability to find cars and believe they can't acquire as many trade-ins as competing dealers.

In this way, the practice of packing cars hurts the used vehicle department's ability to acquire vehicles for the lowest cost and it slows the velocity of both new and used vehicle sales.

The Risks of Reconditioning: There are two long-standing beliefs about used vehicle reconditioning that today's dealers must revisit to ensure they're helping, rather than hurting, the profitability of these cars as they're made ready for the front line.

1. **Charging retail rates for reconditioning work.** I recognize why dealers believe they should charge the used vehicle department retail rates for parts and labor as they repair cars. The practice maximizes the dealer's overall profit potential in fixed operations.

But in today's efficient market, this decision increasingly runs the risk of compressing a dealer's profit margin and, potentially, increasing a vehicle's asking price beyond the "market" for the same or similar cars.

Consider the way CarMax views the relationship between reconditioning costs and profit margins. In its 2012 fiscal year report, the nation's largest used car retailer notes it works diligently to cut reconditioning costs to preserve its profit margin—even as the company's stores, like many dealers, are acquiring older, more beat-up vehicles that need a higher degree of attention and work to make them retail-ready:

> *"Last year, we reported that our efforts to eliminate waste from our used vehicle reconditioning processes in recent years had allowed us to achieve a cumulative, sustainable reduction in average reconditioning costs of approximately $250 per vehicle. Adjusting for an increase in the average age of vehicles reconditioned and sold, we continued to realize $250 per unit in savings in fiscal 2012."*

I am not privy to CarMax's parts and labor costs, but I suspect they are significantly lower than those for franchised dealers. Even more profound, the company is reducing its reconditioning costs while these profit-crimping add-on costs are increasing for many franchised dealers.

In my day as a dealer, it was almost an automatic that a $1 investment in reconditioning would yield a $1.25 return. Today's market, however, is too competitive, efficient and transparent to consider the investment in reconditioning as the near-guarantee it was for me.

As we'll see in upcoming chapters, velocity dealers on the road to reinvention are finding that it's necessary to reduce reconditioning costs to maintain the front-end margins they expect from vehicles. They are addressing this cost pressure by minimizing the scope of reconditioning work and the costs for the parts and labor required to do the job.

The benefit? They see a greater number of internal ROs, albeit at a slightly lower rate, that drives a larger level of overall dealership profit-ability—while retaining the front-end gross profit margin they expect. In other words, they extend and maximize the benefit of velocity management to fixed operations.

2. **Creating accountability for reconditioning delays and mistakes.** Most dealers recognize that delays in reconditioning hurt the overall ROI and profitability they can expect in used vehicles. The problem? When these profit-sapping delays occur, dealers do not hold their service departments accountable. Typically, the used vehicle department gets left holding the bag for the delay-driven, diminished profitability on used vehicles.

This is not the collaborative, win-win scenario that is necessary to maximize the velocity and profitability in both departments. Velocity- and reinvention-focused dealers like my friend Russ Wallace at the Bill Marsh Auto Group, in Traverse City, tackled this problem head-on, crafting new processes to balance the need for reconditioning and profits in service with the need for front-end margin in used vehicles.

A prediction: I believe we'll soon see wider use of pay plans for used vehicle and service departments that do a better job of balancing the risks and rewards that flow from reconditioning used vehicles—and do not solely penalize the used vehicle department when reconditioning delays occur.

It pains me to hear dealers complain about a lack of profitability in used vehicles when they do not fully evaluate their processes for reconditioning and address inefficiencies that reduce their profitability potential.

As I tell my sons, it's okay to complain about a problem, but it's not okay to keep complaining unless you've done everything in your power to correct the issue that ails you.

Speaking of complaining, I'm done with my wake-up call. I hope it's helped you see how some traditional used vehicle management practices harm the investment return and profit-ability potential of their used vehicle operations.

Broadly, the fix for all of these shortcomings follows a decision by dealers to fully regard their used vehicles as investments—and take the necessary steps to protect and preserve the return on their investments they seek and deserve.

Next up: A closer look at how new technology and tools help dealers manage their used vehicles as investments.

A Game-Changer Arrives

When an investment manager takes on a client, there's a requisite round of questions. What's your tolerance for risk? What's your window for a return? What kind of return do you expect to see?

The point of the questions, of course, is to sketch a strategy for investing the client's money. From there, the astute investment manager decides the right mix of investments—small cap stocks, large cap stocks, domestic/foreign, bonds, etc.—to meet the client's goals for risks and rewards.

I would argue today's dealers and used vehicle managers need to take a similar, set-the-strategy approach for their used vehicle inventories. These inventories are, after all, investments. It's the dealer's money. And it's often a seven-figure sum.

Yet, many dealers do not treat their inventories as a bona fide investment. They don't set a strategy. They don't define their own parameters for risk and reward. They don't go to school on their local and regional markets to know, without a doubt, the exact used vehicles and configurations that represent the best possible return on investment (ROI) for their dealerships.

Dealer Tom Ahl of Tom Ahl Family of Dealerships in Lima, Ohio, readily admits that's how he *used* to regard his used vehicle business. For him, it's always been about buying cars that he thinks will work well for his store. He likes the auctions. He likes to buy.

"If there were 300 cars at the auction, I'd want 30 of them," says Ahl, who is celebrating 50 years as a dealer in 2012. "I'd just go from my head and gut on what we've sold before."

For a lot of years, Ahl did well in used vehicles. The Internet changed that. Now, what he thinks might make a good investment can quickly turn to a dud.

"We bought some Lexuses thinking they were great cars," Ahl says. He came back to the dealership and his GM Joe Parent showed him the market data from the dealership's inventory management system.

"There hasn't been a used Lexus sold in this part of Ohio for the past two months anywhere other than a Lexus dealership," Ahl says. "I've got one over

there I've had for six months. I can't get anybody
to look at it.

"It's a 2008. It's red. It drives perfectly. 27,000 miles.
It looks pretty to me. Evidently everybody else
knows you don't buy those things if you're not a
Lexus dealer," Ahl says with a laugh.

I share Tom's story to make two points. First, his
instinct-driven approach to acquiring cars illustrates the traditional way many dealers have fed
their used vehicle inventories. Second, his road to
reinvention in used vehicles now includes a clear-
cut strategy, one that helps him resist the innate
urge to raise his hand at auctions when he likes a
car.

"The business has changed a lot." Ahl says. "You
can't just go buy a pretty car and look at the
book and see if it's in range and think you're okay.
There's too many other parameters involved."

Ahl's strategy is driven by his adoption of a more
strategic, investment-oriented approach to used
vehicle acquisitions. Today, Ahl isn't just buying
cars to stock his inventory. He now recognizes each
vehicle acquisition is really a decision to provision
his dealership's cash and resources to ensure the
highest possible ROI for every used car.

Ahl and Parent rely on velocity-based metrics (e.g.,
market days supply, cost to market and price to
market) to guide these investment decisions and
help them provision the appropriate level of money

and resources to enhance the value of the investment (e.g., reconditioning) and set the stage for a quick return (e.g., online merchandising/pricing and sales processes).

This concept of treating used vehicles as investments and provisioning resources to achieve an acceptable ROI came about during the product development brainstorming sessions in Atlanta with developers from vAuto, AutoTrader.com and Manheim.

We recognized that the volatility and efficiency of today's used vehicle marketplace means dealers like Ahl need more than just paint-sharp instincts to make sound used vehicle investment decisions. We also recognized dealers needed better technology and tools to ensure they provisioned the "right" amount of attention, energy and resources to improve and protect each used vehicle's investment return and profitability potential from the moment of acquisition to its eventual sale.

As we brainstormed, it became clear that dealers and used vehicle managers needed a system much like the portfolio management programs investment managers use to keep track of their client preferences and goals, and to guide buy/sell decisions that would maximize investment returns and meet client expectations.

vAuto's new Provision® inventory management system brings all this together: It distills market data into management metrics that dealers and used vehicle managers use to easily and quickly understand the risks and rewards inherent in every vehicle. Further, the system helps them efficiently and effectively manage and maximize each vehicle's investment potential from the moment of acquisition to the moment of sale.

The foundation for this new provisioning approach to managing used vehicles is the belief that used vehicles are, in fact, significant investments for dealers. I believe this approach, and the new technology and tools that surround it, are a game-changer for dealers.

For the first time, they have a bird's-eye view of real-time indicators of every vehicle's investment potential. In addition, they now have the data, metrics and technology to easily, efficiently and effectively manage each vehicle's investment return.

Of course, as I noted above, dealers can't fully leverage the benefits of this new approach until they understand how to set a strategy that will drive the provisioning of resources to maximize the investment return and profitability potential for each vehicle.

Let's now address how to establish this used vehicle investment strategy.

ESTABLISHING YOUR INVENTORY INVESTMENT STRATEGY

A used vehicle investment strategy for dealers begins with identifying the types of investments that work best for a dealership and its market.

Like the choices investment managers make about stocks and bonds, dealers need to determine the types of vehicle segments that offer the best investment potential. These segments should be viewed as the "strategic hotspots" in a market.

These "hotspots" are based on vehicle segments, rather than specific vehicle makes and models. The rationale for this follows the strategic logic an investment manager would apply to a client's portfolio: Before I can begin picking specific stocks and bonds as investments, I need to determine the class or type of investment that offers the best opportunity to achieve a client's investment goals.

This is the strategic thinking my friend Russ Wallace at the Bill Marsh Auto Group, Traverse City, displayed on his dry-erase boards.

Russ helped me understand that vehicle segments (compact, sedan, SUV, truck, etc.) are the used-vehicle-equivalent to a class of investments (e.g., stocks, bonds, etc.). These strategic "hotspots" vary from market to market, and dealership to dealership.

For example, a Jaguar dealer in Texas might make a strategic decision to limit his investment in pick-up trucks, even though the Lone Star state is generally regarded as a truck-friendly market. This strategic decision would likely owe more to the dealer's desire to position the store as an outlet for luxury vehicles.

In this scenario, the Jaguar dealer probably wouldn't shy away from selling a good-looking, well-appointed truck it acquired on a trade-in. But the dealer would also likely limit efforts to buy trucks at auctions, preferring to focus those acquisition efforts on supporting the dealership's strategic identity as a luxury car retailer.

Here is how the Provision® inventory management system helps dealers identify these "strategic hotspots" and craft an inventory investment strategy that fits their dealership goals and local market potential. This work begins with two broad strategy-oriented stakes:

Strategic Stake 1. Determine the types of investments, or used vehicle segments, that best fit your brand, your market and your dealership's goals for inventory turn, profitability and sales volumes. Provision provides market demand and sales data to help dealers identify these segments based on their respective rates of sale in the market and the dealer's own used vehicle sales history and retail preferences.

Provision presents each segment as cells on a strategy page, allowing dealers to activate or deactivate the segments they determine are most appropriate for their investment goals in used vehicle operations.

For example, the chart on page 68 shows a dealer who has "turned on" each vehicle segment based on market data and the dealership's retailing preferences. This dealer's preferences are likely to be much different than the Jaguar dealer in Texas, who might shut off the truck and van segments.

Like investment managers, dealers should recognize that these strategic "hotspots" can change, depending on market volatility and seasonality.

For example, the dealer represented by the chart might shut off trucks and SUVs if and when gas prices spike and demand for the larger vehicles

Inventory Preferences

			$10k-15k	$15k-20k	$20k-25k
☑	🚗	Subcompact	◯	◯	◯
☑	🚗	Sport	◯	◯	◯
☑	🚗	Intermediate	◯	◯	◯
☑	🚙	SUV	◯	◯	◯
☑	🛻	Truck	◯	◯	◯
☑	🚐	Van	◯	◯	◯

wanes. Or, during winter months, this dealer might eliminate sports cars given the lower seasonal demand.

A recommendation: Dealers should revisit these strategic allocations on at least a quarterly basis to ensure they fit changing market conditions.

This initial strategic stake is the first step velocity dealers take on the road to reinvention. It's a stepping stone to guide a more efficient and market-focused approach to truly managing their used vehicle inventories as investments.

Strategic Stake 2: Determine how much to invest in each vehicle segment or "strategic hotspot" in your market area. This strategic prong reflects the allocation of investments an investment manager would perform for a client—$X goes here, $Y goes here, and so on.

The Provision system helps dealers address this strategic stake by allocating the number of vehicles (known as the dealership days supply) they should carry in each vehicle segment to meet market demand and their goals for inventory turn and sales volumes. Provision recognizes that each "strategic hotspot" should feature vehicles at multiple price points to meet prevailing buyer demands in a specific market (see chart below).

Inventory Preferences

		$10k-15k	$15k-20k	$20k-25k
☐	Subcompact	◯	◯	◯
☐	Sport	◯	◯	◯
☑	Intermediate	45	45	45
☑	SUV	45	45	45
☑	Truck	45	45	45
☐	Van	◯	◯	◯

The Provision system's dealer-focused flexibility also recognizes that dealers must make choices—both to reflect their preferences as retailers as well as the inherent limits on the size of the investment they can allocate to each vehicle segment or "strategic hotspot."

The dealer in our chart has opted to focus his used vehicle operations strategy on three vehicle segments—intermediate sedans, SUVs and trucks. Similarly, the dealer has determined that a 45-day dealership days supply in each segment, as well as each segment's price groups, is the correct, market-focused allocation to match his goals for used vehicle inventory turns, sales volumes and composition.

With both of these strategic stakes firmly planted, the Provision system then does two things. First, it helps dealers balance their inventory needs to match the strategy they've set for the placement and allocation of their used vehicle investment. Like an investment manager's portfolio management software, Provision makes recommendations to buy and sell vehicles within each "strategic hotspot" as dealers need to replace units they've sold or get rid of vehicles to balance the days supply to fit the strategic objective.

The chart on page 71 shows Provision's buy and sell recommendations for a dealer in Wisconsin who has tweaked his inventory strategy to prepare for winter, loading up on SUVs and easing his allocation of trucks. In the SUV segment, for example, the decision to increase the dealership days supply to 60 days means the dealer needs to acquire more vehicles across each segment's price bands. In trucks, the dealer's decision to ease the dealership days supply now translates to Provision-driven recommendations to sell existing inventory to balance the dealer's strategic goals.

Target Dealership Days Supply

			$10k-15k	$15k-20k	$20k-25k
☐	🚗	Subcompact	◯	◯	◯
☐	🚗	Sport	◯	◯	◯
☑	🚗	Intermediate	(45) +2	(45) +1	(45) -2
☑	🚙	SUV	(60) +6	(60) +8	(60) +5
☑	🛻	Truck	(30) 0	(30) -1	(30) -4
☐	🚐	Van	◯	◯	◯

Both of these Provision-driven strategic stakes ensure dealers have a baseline strategy for their used vehicle inventory investment, as well as a framework for more efficient, effective and market-focused inventory management decisions.

I firmly believe dealers can no longer operate in today's competitive and volatile used vehicle retail environment without a strategy. My conviction here is the chief reason Provision and its strategy-setting functionality exist—an investment-based and market-focused strategy for used vehicle investments and management decisions is essential for dealers to survive and prosper.

So far, many velocity dealers who have adopted the Provision system's strategic precepts agree it's the "game-changer" I thought it could be during those initial brainstorming sessions in Atlanta.

"The worst thing you can do is say, 'we're going to put as many cars out there as we think we need,'" says dealer Mike Marsh of the Bill Marsh Auto Group, Traverse City. "You have to manage to a number. By managing to a number, it becomes a discipline to find the right mix. Provision helps you identify and track the best inventory, with the highest velocity and profitability."

Marsh's comment highlights a critical point: It's not okay for dealers and used vehicle managers to lack a strategy for their investment in used vehicles. Likewise, once you have a strategy, it's unacceptable not to apply yourself at work, every day, to ensure all of your inventory decisions reflect the strategy you've established at your dealership.

In my personal life, I have an investment manager who handles my money. I presume that, on a daily basis, he's evaluating the marketplace to determine how to allocate my money to meet my goals for the highest possible return with the lowest amount of risk. If I learn he's not paying attention to market dynamics, and my returns suffer, you can bet I'll make a phone call. I might even fire him in favor of someone else who is more diligent about serving my needs as an investor.

Increasingly, this is the kind of accountability dealers should expect from their used vehicle managers. They should be both the architects and stewards of the dealer's investment strategy in used vehicles. As such, it's also their responsibility to execute this strategy every day, making the right asset allocations and buy/sell decisions, just as an investment manager would for a client.

The good news for these used vehicle managers: Today's inventory management technology and tools make the job of executing the dealer's used vehicle investment strategy easier and more efficient than it used to be.

(7)

EXECUTING YOUR USED VEHICLE INVENTORY INVESTMENT STRATEGY

Wouldn't it be cool if used cars could talk to you?

"Mr. Dealer, I'm a two-year-old Accord. All my brothers and sisters are certified. I'm not. I really don't think I should be here."

"Mr. Dealer, I know I'm a spiffy, sleek black BMW 325i. People always talk about how good I look on test drives. Time and again, though, they ask about heated seats, which I don't have. I think this might be a problem."

"Mr. Dealer, I'm a hard-working, honest Ford F-150. I hate to ask, but could you lower my price? I just don't think, given my mileage and condition, I've ever been worth as much as you think."

This is one of the concepts I brought to the brainstorming table in Atlanta.

I knew that the AutoTrader.com's voting machine contained a treasure trove of data that neither I, nor any dealers, had seen before.

My goal was to develop technology and tools that would tabulate this market intelligence and help dealers establish and execute their used vehicle inventory investment strategy. I believed that it could and should be possible for dealers to know, with great precision, all of the elements that make up the value proposition for every used vehicle. These innovations would help dealers recognize and adjust for the inherent opportunities and risks each car posed for their investment strategy.

I think the end result, as embodied in Provision, is pretty cool. It makes the job of executing a dealer's used vehicle investment strategy easier. It also helps dealers and used vehicle managers achieve greater efficiencies in people and processes to drive bigger returns on their used vehicle investments.

THE ESSENTIAL "3 W's" OF INVENTORY MANAGEMENT

I've always loved this quote from the Italian master painter, inventor and thinker, Leonardo da Vinci: "Simplicity is the ultimate sophistication."

This is a particularly powerful insight for anyone who seeks to develop technology and tools to help car dealers become more efficient, effective and profitable retailers. If dealers can't readily see how a new system will help them cut costs, sell more cars and make more money, chances are better than good they won't sign up.

This is why the Provision system's technology and tools to help dealers and used vehicle managers execute their used vehicle investment strategy aim for simplicity. The entire execute-the-strategy functionality is based on what I call the "3 W's" of inventory management—what cars to buy? what to pay? and where to find them efficiently and quickly?

What Cars to Buy? Provision answers this question through its innovative Report Card, which assigns an A-F letter grade to each of the seven factors that make up each vehicle's unique investment proposition (see box, next page).

The Report Card embodies the "talking cars" concept I introduced in Atlanta. Armed with the voting

7 Factors of Used Vehicle Desirability

Here are the seven factors that the Provision Report Card grades to help dealers listen to what their used vehicles and markets are saying:

Demand: Distills the number of shoppers searching for a specific car in a dealer's market.

Interest: Reveals the average SRP to VDP conversion for a specific vehicle in a dealer's market area.

Volume: Measures the sales rate or number of recent sales for a specific vehicle in a dealer's market.

Days Supply: Shows the number of similarly equipped vehicles available in a dealer's market and its daily retail sales rate in the past 45 days. Lower days supply means higher demand/profit/turn potential.

Profitability: Measures the "spread" between the acquisition cost and average retail price for a vehicle, after accounting for transportation, reconditioning and other costs.

Availability: Assesses the number of vehicles available in the wholesale market.

Experience: Measures a dealership's success selling a specific vehicle by make/model/trim.

machine data from AutoTrader.com and velocity-based market data and metrics, Provision's Report Card informs dealers of the investment opportunities and risks for every car in real time, no matter the make/model or equipment/trim configuration.

The Report Card works in conjunction with the strategic, investment-focused stakes dealers plant in the Provision system. As dealers map their preferred strategic vehicle segments and dealership days supply targets, the system identifies and recommends vehicles that fit these segments and price parameters.

Dealers can then review these vehicles through the Report Card—and in an instant, they see an overall letter grade for a car, as well as individual grades for each of the seven factors that determine a vehicle's desirability in the market. In other words, Provision provides a more efficient and precise way to determine whether a vehicle is "right" for a dealer's inventory and investment strategy.

This is how the Provision Report Card "talks" to dealers about what's right and wrong with every car.

It knows if the Accord's certification is a problem for a non-Honda dealer; it's aware of the BMW buyer's preference for heated seats; and it knows exactly if the F-150's pricing is out of line with the market. In fact, the Report Card would have warned dealer Tom Ahl to stay away from that red 2008 Lexus.

Velocity dealers say the Report Card adds confidence to their used vehicle investment decisions.

"I need to know the full package on every car—how many people are searching for it, its scarcity in the market, everything," affirms Marc Ray, vice president and partner at Grogan's Towne Chrysler, Toledo. "Provision gives me the full package to make the right decisions. There's no guesswork anymore on what the 'right' cars will be. I'm definitely making fewer mistakes."

For each of the seven factors, the Provision system assigns a default weighting. This weighting reflects the velocity philosophy for turning-and-earning used vehicles to maximize a dealer's return on investment (ROI). For example, the Report Card gives more weight to the forward-looking "demand" and "interest" factors than a dealer's past "experience." This owes to my belief that market history has less relevance for what will happen tomorrow than real-time indicators that offer a sneak peek at where the market's heading.

Even so, Provision gives dealers the ability to adjust these weightings to fit their specific preferences as retailers.

For example, Trent Waybright, used vehicle director at the six-store Kelley Automotive Group, Fort Wayne, Indiana, dialed up the weighting for "experience." The rationale: They do extremely well with General Motors products and want the Provision system to proffer every GM car that might present an opportunity.

Other reasons dealers may adjust the Report Card factor weighting:

- A dealer who wants to increase inventory turns and sales volumes could increase the weightings for the "demand" and "interest" factors to spot the specific vehicles that will be fast-sellers given the online attention from in-market shoppers.

- If a dealer wants to increase front-end gross profits, he could increase the weighting of the "profitability" factor to identify vehicles that have the best "spread" between their costs to own the car and its likely retail price point. This decision would increase the chances to find "home run" cars and/or function as a hedge against internal pressures on the "spread," such as the costs for reconditioning and packs.

As dealers specify their preferences for the types of vehicles that will work best for their dealerships, the Provision system balances these against the strategic stakes they've set for their inventories. From there, Provision generates a "shopping list" that recommends specific, letter-graded vehicles dealers use to acquire cars to replenish the "strategic hotspots" they've established for their overall inventories.

The "shopping list" (see image, this page) displays these recommended cars with a vehicle identification number and details color, mileage, condition and any auction seller notes about the vehicle.

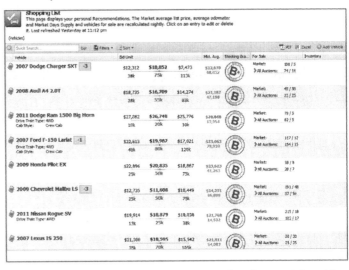

Dealers and their buyers can use this list to identify the vehicles that are "right" for their inventory and investment parameters.

What to Pay? Every dealer knows the age-old axiom, "you make your profit when you buy a used car." This has never been more true than today, as we've seen wholesale prices climb higher and retail prices contract, creating compression on the dealer's investment margin, or "spread," in used vehicles.

To address this critical point in the profitability equation for dealers, Provision provides bid guidance to dealers to ensure the amounts they pay for a vehicle at auctions or trade-ins are "on the money" for the current market and their ROI goal for each vehicle.

The bid guidance conjoins several important factors—the likely wholesale auction acquisition cost, the dealer's expected reconditioning, transportation and pack costs, the dealer's ROI or gross profit goal for the car, and the prevailing retail asking price for the same or similar vehicles (see image, this page). In short, the bid guidance tells dealers "what to pay" up front to help them efficiently and effectively manage the "spread" on a vehicle and give the car its best shot to achieve a dealer's ROI objective.

Where to Find the Vehicles Quickly and Efficiently?

Thanks to the participation of AutoTrader.com, Manheim, Adesa, GMAC, SmartAuction and other auctions, the Provision system is the industry's first to integrate access to real-time wholesale auction run lists and bidding platforms across the country.

It works like this: Once dealers have evaluated Provision's recommended vehicles through the Report Card grading system, and assess the system's bid guidance on these cars, they can click-through to auctions and place proxy bids or deploy buyers to the exact lanes where these "right" vehicles will run.

Dealers say this direct-to-auction access is a godsend, given today's highly competitive used vehicle wholesale marketplace. They offer this feedback for two reasons:

1. **It's far more efficient than manual cross-checks of dealership buy lists and auction run lists.** "This is a huge efficiency gain for us," Waybright says. "Before Provision, we were spending eight hours each week with spreadsheets to match our buy lists to vehicles at specific auctions. Now the matching is automatic."

2. **Proxy bids matter more.** In early 2012, Manheim reports they've seen a near-doubling of proxy bids from dealers looking to purchase used vehicles. This increase owes to the current crimp in used vehicle supplies that has followed the economic downturn, as well as the increased competition among dealers to find cars to feed their inventories. Provision's integration with national auctions and their bidding platforms is intended to speed the efficiencies and efficacy of this part of the vehicle acquisition process for dealers. A prediction: This integration will only become more complete and efficiency-focused as vAuto continues to partner with auction service providers to increase Provision's vehicle acquisition value proposition for dealers.

As dealers use the Provision system, they find it is an invaluable tool for establishing and executing an investment-minded used vehicle inventory strategy.

Beyond this, though, many velocity dealers use Provision as the central hub to drive and oversee their respective roads to reinvention and efficiencies in used vehicles and other dealership departments.

This faith in the Provision system stands to reason.

As I mentioned earlier, Provision is built with a return on a dealer's used vehicle investment in mind. From an acquisition perspective, Provision offers an early-warning of potential risks to a vehicle's investment potential. While a used vehicle is part of a dealer's inventory, Provision provides real-time tracking of the health of the dealer's investment in the car. In this way, Provision is a "red alert"-type system that flags dealers and used vehicle managers when the return they expect may be at risk.

I'm not suggesting the Provision system is an all-knowing system, but it comes pretty close.

Not surprisingly, as velocity dealers use Provision and attune their used vehicle inventories and operations to meet the needs of their investment strategy, the people and process inefficiencies in other departments become extremely problematic.

I call these roadblocks to reinvention. Sometimes, these spur painful and profound change in dealerships.

We'll spend the next several chapters addressing how velocity dealers have bumped into and broken through each roadblock—all in the name of protecting, preserving and pumping up the dealer's ROI in used vehicles.

REINVENTION ROADBLOCK:
DEALERSHIP DEPARTMENT SILOS

There's always been a "to each his own" mentality in car dealerships.

In Sales: A manager holds the line with a customer who wants a $1,000 discount on a new vehicle deal, refusing to reduce the asking price more than $500. To keep the customer happy, however, the manager adds $500 to the value of the customer's trade-in. The manager may recognize the decision hurts the trade-in's return on investment (ROI) potential for the dealership, but it's not his problem. He did his job to "hold gross" for the new vehicle department.

In Service: A service manager gives top priority to retail customers. He instructs technicians to always work on those vehicles first, never mind the line of used cars that need reconditioning. He may recognize the customer-first priority hurts the used vehicle department, and the dealer's ROI potential of every car, but it's not his problem. He's doing his job to ensure top customer satisfaction ratings and maintain his customer-pay dollars per repair order (RO) ratio.

In Parts: A parts director refuses to prime the service department with the parts it may need for a given day's appointments. He may recognize the decision slows a technician's productivity while waiting for parts, but it's not his problem. He's doing exactly what he's been taught to do, and has done for years.

In F&I: An F&I manager reworks a deal to pay for the sale of a service contract to a customer. He may recognize the decision shrinks the front-end gross on the deal, but it's not his problem. He's done his job to maintain the department's warranty penetration rate and gross profits.

Each of these scenarios happens every day in dealerships across the country. They are all signs of the "to each his own" culture that many traditional dealers still regard as the best way to do business.

But let's not pull any punches. This culture, and the self-focused decision-making it spawns, does not work anymore.

For starters, it creates what business management consultants would call a "silo effect." This occurs when an organization lacks shared focus and purpose:

> The phrase "silo effect," popular in the business and organizational communities, refers to a lack of communication and common goals between departments in an organization. It is the opposite of systems thinking in an organization. The silo effect gets its name from the farm storage silo; each silo is designated for one specific grain.[3]

In the car business, the "silo effect" is alive and well—and many dealers still believe it's a good thing.

It's hard to blame them. They were brought up to regard each dealership department as its own unique business. Each department stood or fell on its own merits. Managers were strictly paid off the gross profits they generated in their respective departments. Competition between departments (and the occasional fistfight in the sales office) was considered a good thing.

---

[3] http://en.wikipedia.org/wiki/Information_silo

The problem here is that the "silo effect" breeds inefficiencies and undermines the intra-department collaboration and cooperation that is now necessary for dealers to maximize the investment potential and profitability of their business.

In fact, the "silo effect" is one of the first roadblocks dealers encounter on the road to reinvention as they begin their journey to maximize efficiencies and their ROI in used vehicles.

This is due to the recognition that improving the velocity of sales, ROI and profitability in used vehicles requires a carefully planned synergy between every department in the dealership.

"Used cars really cut across the entire dealership, unlike anything else," says dealer David Hudson of the five-store group, Hudson Automotive, Madisonville, Ky. "A rising tide lifts all boats. That's what it did for us."

Hudson's referring to the near-doubling of used vehicle volumes at his dealerships following a conscious decision to maximize his investment in used vehicles by focusing on process efficiencies and tackling any signs or symptoms of the "silo effect" that would slow his progress and potential.

At his Charleston, S.C., store, for example, Hudson notes that synergies between the used vehicle and other departments has brought significant improvement to the dealership's ability to sell used vehicles and drive more profitability in every department.

"It literally changed our whole business," Hudson says. "When you recondition 145 cars a month versus 40, the impact in service and parts is unbelievable. Then you're selling more in F&I and improving your throughput on new vehicles, because you can pay more for trades."

Hudson recognizes the "silo effect" is detrimental to his ability as a dealer to maximize his investment and profitability potential.

"I want harmony in the dealerships," Hudson says. "I want the most gross I can get for the least expense in every department. Using pay plans to keep that in line is important." His approach: All managers in new/used vehicle sales and F&I are paid from variable gross profits; parts and services managers share gross profits from those departments, or fixed operations.

Dealer Keith Kocourek of Wausau, Wis., shares the belief that synergy beats silos any day.

As he's reinvented his dealerships with a central focus on used vehicles, Kocourek has made impressive gains in sales and profitability. He's not just cranking up used vehicle sales, he's lighting up every department.

'I want to make $30,000 in net profit for every $100,000 of gross profit," he says. "That's tough for a guy to do these days but we're hitting the mark on a regular basis."

I like the analogy Kocourek uses to describe all this: It's like a wheel. The hub is the used vehicle department. The spokes are all the processes that surround every used vehicle touch point in every department—parts, service, F&I and sales departments.

"The wheel starts spinning slowly," Kocourek says. "It starts spinning more. Then, it's almost like it's spinning on its own, going downhill. Once the momentum gets going, it's pretty incredible."

Based on Kocourek's rise as a dealer in recent years, I would go a little further in describing this in-dealership dynamic. It's really a "wheel of fortune" and it's been very good to Kocourek.

Two years ago, he owned two stores doing $90 million in revenue. Today, Kocourek has five stores that average about 350 used and 150 new vehicle sales each month. He's on pace to hit $160 million in revenue in 2012. His used vehicle inventory turns 15 to 16 times a year, and the average age of his used vehicles is 24 days. His overall dealership net profits are up 72 percent in the past two years, and, like Hudson, he's got an appetite for more acquisition opportunities.

"Our competitors are scratching their heads and wondering what's next," Kocourek says. "We can sell a used car for $300 less than them and make $200 more. It's the reason we've been able to grow and buy out the competition."

When I see the success of guys like Kocourek and Hudson, I wonder why other dealers do not yet see the inefficiencies the "silo effect" creates for their dealerships, and the "wheel of fortune" they're sometimes painfully missing. After all, every dealership has the same combination of fixed and variable departments, and the opportunity to reinvent their processes and profitability in used vehicles and beyond.

I took this question to Tony Allison, a dealer accountant and partner at Crowe Horwath LLC, South Bend, Ind. He leads 20 Group roundtables for chief financial officers at dealerships.

"A big part of the resistance is the mentality of the gross per unit," Allison says. "Some dealers look at gross per unit and that's all they look at. They're not measuring the right thing a lot of times."

This plays both to tradition, and to the type of individual at the helm of a dealership, he adds.

"It depends on the financial sophistication of the dealer and their willingness to learn and listen to maximize their entire business," Allison says. "It also depends on how they came up in the business. If you have a guy who came up in the service and parts business, he's more likely going to be focused on the service and parts business.

"If you have a guy who came up in new cars they will be focused on the new car business," he continues. "That's what he knows and what he grew up with. Then, there are other guys who don't have the ability or interest to broaden their view of things."

A-ha! There we have the root causes for the "silo effect" and "wheel of fortune" problem at dealerships.

In some cases, the dealer's own DNA will seed the "silo effect." In other cases, a dealer's fixation on "gross per unit," rather than the "total gross" that might be generated by every deal, feeds the "silo effect" and inability to see a dealership's innate "wheel of fortune" potential.

"If you increase the volume and the total gross you can drive from used vehicles, you're probably going to be better off than looking at the gross on each deal," Allison says. "You've got to hit more singles and score more runs."

Given the emphasis many dealers place on the average gross per unit, it's worth taking a closer look at why this management metric limits a dealer's ability to hit more singles, put the "wheel of fortune" in motion and ensure every used vehicle delivers maximum ROI for their dealership.

REINVENTION ROADBLOCK: A FIXATION ON AVERAGE FRONT-END GROSS

As I've evangelized the benefits of the investment-minded velocity method of used vehicle inventory management, I've taken some shots.

"Dale Pollak is the prophet of low gross profits."

"That velocity deal…you might sell more cars but it'll kill your grosses."

"vAuto is just a pricing tool that hurts your front-end grosses."

I've taken these shots in stride. To me, the comments were more reflexive than reflective—a "kill the messenger" reaction rather than an attempt to truly understand the message.

To be clear, my message has been consistent, both in substance and relevance for today's dealers: Front-end gross profits are only a part of what it takes to be successful as used vehicle retailers in today's more margin-compressed and price-transparent environment. The real profitability and return on investment (ROI) in used cars comes from the sum of the efficiencies dealers achieve in every department as they increase the volume and velocity of their sales.

In short, dealers should fixate and focus on "total gross" versus "average front-end gross" to turn the "wheel of fortune" at their dealerships and achieve a greater degree of success.

This can be a difficult message for more tradition-minded dealers to hear, much less embrace. The traditional dealership organizational structure, the bulk of its processes, pay plans, and its people are geared to "go for the front-end gross."

For these stores, my investment-focused message will often fall flat because a) it upends long-standing beliefs about the importance of front-end gross profits and, b) it signals a need for profound change and re-tooling in dealerships.

In upcoming chapters, we'll spend a lot of time discussing the mechanics and specifics of the process and people changes dealers on the road to reinvention have undertaken as they've embraced an investment-focused approach to their used vehicle operations.

For now, let's take a closer look at why I've come to regard dealers' tradition-based fixation on front-end gross profits as problematic for profitability:

1. **It diminishes the velocity of inventory turns.** In Chapter 4, we discussed how dealers will say "a little age is okay" as they hold onto vehicles to achieve their front-end gross profit goals. We noted how dealers often fail to fully account for the depreciation of aging inventory that would shrink their front-end gross profits if they applied an honest, investment-oriented accounting methodology.

   Now, let's address how this fixation on average front-end gross profits actually reduces "total gross:" It slows your inventory turn and means fewer opportunities to acquire and retail fresh cars.

   Scott James, chief operating officer for Denver-based Mike Shaw Automotive, notes that while the seven-store dealer group has increased used vehicle sales by 59 percent in the past two years, gross profits have also increased. They now average $1,500 to $1,600 per vehicle, depending on the dealership.

   "The difference is having nothing but fresh cars," says Scott, who notes the group averages

20 inventory turns a year with little to no age issues. "It's the old adage that fresh cars make the most money. Another piece is that when you realize you can turn those cars fast, you're able to get more aggressive on your trades and you sell more new cars. That's how the wheel starts spinning."

"We're far more interested in turn than gross," says Mike Anderson, general manager for Mike Patton Auto Group, LaGrange, Ga. "We average about $1,500 in front-end gross. I want to do that 125 to 150 times a month. I love it when we acquire a car right and it gives you $4,500 up front. But the reality is those cars are really few and far between."

2. **It makes pricing less transparent.** Dealers who fixate on front-end gross margins will typically add a $3,000 to $4,000 mark-up to their vehicles, irrespective of their acquisition costs or prevailing retail prices. In addition to reducing the vehicle's appeal to price-conscious online buyers, this practice makes it difficult for salespeople to offer a rational, believable explanation for the dealership's pricing policies.

"The majority of customers don't mind you making some money as dealers," says dealer David Hudson of Hudson Automotive, Madisonville, Ky. "They don't mind paying $1,000 in profit if they think that's fair and reasonable after they've done some research. But they definitely don't want to be the customer that got rolled over and paid $5,000 too much."

We'll examine pricing and sales techniques in an upcoming chapter that centers on "documentation as the new negotiation." Dealers are using these methods to achieve their front-end gross profit goals *and* convey a greater degree of honesty and transparency in their pricing.

3. **It masks profit-draining inefficiencies.** There's a correlation between the degree of a dealer's fixation on front-end gross profits and his ability to identify and address process and people inefficiencies that diminish the profitability and ROI potential in used vehicles.

For example, if a dealer is willing to hold on to a vehicle for 90 days or more to achieve a "home run" front-end gross profit, the chances are better than good this dealer isn't likely to mind a seven-to-10-day turnaround for reconditioning used vehicles. The same goes for multi-day lags in posting a used vehicle's description and photos online.

By contrast, dealers who regard their used vehicles as investments recognize time is money in today's environment. As they monitor the velocity management metrics, they can clearly see how such delays crimp their ability to turn their inventory quickly and translate to lost opportunities, less ROI and lower overall profitability.

My message here is not that a dealer's front-end gross profit average doesn't matter. It does, and dealers should do everything in their power to improve their front-end margins as much as possible.

But let's be clear: Front-end gross profits are only part of the "total gross" equation that will ultimately maximize a dealer's used vehicle ROI and profitability. The more a dealer fixates on average front-end gross, the less likely he will be able to reinvent the processes and people necessary to increase the "total gross" and ROI contribution every used vehicle can deliver for the dealership.

REINVENTION IN ACTION:
METRICS, METAL AND HARMONY

The phone rings in Trent Waybright's office at the Kelley Automotive Group.

The caller is Chuck Kelley, the general manager of the six-store group's Chevrolet store in Fort Wayne, Ind., and cousin to dealer Tom Kelley.

Chuck Kelley wants to ask Waybright, head of used vehicle operations at Kelley, about an appraisal for a 2007 Buick LaCrosse his store had taken in as a trade on a new vehicle deal.

"Trent? Help educate me again," Kelley says via speakerphone. "I'm trying to find out whether we appraised a car light or strong. It's a 2007 Buick LaCrosse. They appraised it at the SuperStore a month ago for $11,500. We just delivered the new car. We never saw the LaCrosse until it showed up. I drove it home to check it out. It drove real nice but seemed to have a growl in the power steering. I'm not looking for more money, I'm just wondering how you think we appraised the car."

Waybright guides Kelley to the car in the group's used vehicle inventory management system. He shows Kelley how the car is "right" for the dealership's inventory, given the system recommends two vehicles to fill the LaCrosse's inventory segment.

But, the system also offers a "C" letter grade on the car due to its mileage and competing vehicles.

"$11,500 seems like plenty of money," Waybright tells Kelley. "It has a bad CarFax, 81,000 miles and it has problems. It's probably a $10,500 piece, maybe $11,000."

"Hmmm…how many other cars are like it in the market?" Kelley asks.

Waybright walks Kelley through a series of mouse-clicks to identify competing cars. There are several in the immediate area, and the metrics show none are fast-sellers.

"I see," Kelley says. "There's four just like it and one's 79 days old, another's 81 days and another's 229 days. That's very interesting."

"You're getting there, Chuck," Waybright says.

"Well, I haven't arrived but I'm better than I once was," Kelley says.

They both laugh, and Kelley promises to send Waybright the reconditioning estimate for the LaCrosse.

"Don't have them do the repairs," Waybright says. "I want to do a little more research first."

"Sounds good, Trent. Thank you."

As Waybright hangs up the phone, he makes a to-do note for himself. He's going to more thoroughly assess the LaCrosse's potential as retail-oriented investment, and he's going to chat with the appraiser.

"Our salespeople can sell from any store," Waybright explains to me after the call. "Ideally they'll communicate with the store that will get the trade-in. It's their car, after all.

"We have a new policy coming out that makes me the mediator," he adds. "If a store calls me with a trade-in that nobody knows about, I'll look at it. If the store's buried in the car, the appraising store will eat the difference. It'll happen once and the problem will be over."

Bingo, I thought. The stories I'd heard about the "everyone-on-board" approach to velocity management metrics and principles at the Kelley group appeared to be true. I mean, if a veteran car guy with family ties to the dealer is calling Waybright to figure out potential return on investment (ROI) problems on an appraisal, it's pretty clear all the oars at the dealership are rowing together.

I've come to Fort Wayne to see the results of an ROI-focused reinvention effort that dealer Tom Kelley launched about two and a half years ago. At the time, his thinking about used vehicles took a step forward. He'd hit a growing pain as a velocity dealer. He'd been pricing vehicles with the market and his ROI in mind, but his dealerships hadn't fully reinvented other stages of a used vehicle's life cycle to ensure ROI every step of the way.

In some ways, the troubles were bi-products of the "silo effect" and "fixation on front-end gross" discussed in the prior chapters. Kelley was selling cars and turning his inventory, but he wasn't making all of the money he could. Issues like the appraisal on the 2007 LaCrosse occurred too frequently.

"We were fumbling a bit," Waybright says. "We were trying to increase the turn but we didn't have the acquisition part of it figured out.

"TK said, 'We're going to do this. We're going to have a strategy. I'd rather not have enough inventory and own it properly, than have just the right amount or more just sitting there,'" he adds. "Since then, we've gone all in."

This ROI-focused reinvention effort led to a centralized used vehicle operations department that oversees the acquisition and pricing of every used car in Kelley's 300-unit inventory. Today, the dealer group is selling slightly fewer cars (3,417 in 2011 compared to 3,762 in 2009) and making more money.

"We've increased net profit more than 70 percent, just in our pre-owned department," says Waybright, noting the group seeks to turns its inventory 15-plus times a year. "We've had a $500,000 swing in wholesale losses and don't really lose anything anymore. It's a credit to the centralized approach to acquiring vehicles and managing our inventory.

"We've worked very hard to get here," he adds. "Metrics-wise we do well in a lot of categories. Our challenge now is to go to the next level and achieve even more volume and profitability."

Here's a quick look at some of the "good stuff" Waybright has helped implement to ensure the dealer group acquires the "right" cars for the "right" money and prices them to maximize the ROI on every used vehicle:

Centralized, metrics-disciplined acquisitions: Way-bright's office sits across from what might be called the "buying room." It houses a three-person buying team. This trio scours online and physical auctions for vehicles to feed inventories at each of Kelley's six dealerships. They are looking for vehicles that fit the strategic metrics and parameters Waybright has established for each of the group's dealerships.

"There are no emotions attached to any car, whether it's our purchasing or exit strategy," he says.

The central acquisition team aims to acquire vehicles, whether via auction or trade-in, at a target cost to market of 82 percent to 83 percent, provided their mileage meets the retail market average.

If a vehicle's mileage is higher than the average, the team aims for a 75 percent to 77 percent cost to market ratio when they acquire the car. The rationale: The cars are less desirable, will likely require more reconditioning and will require aggressive pricing to overcome their less-than-ideal condition.

By contrast, the cost to market target is 87 percent for vehicles with lower-than-average mileage. The thinking: The cars are likely more desirable and require less reconditioning. Likewise, the mileage and condition may allow a higher retail asking price.

In addition to these metrics, the buyers also weigh a vehicle's market days supply and demand index metrics to ensure they account for all the relevant factors before determining the appropriate acquisition price for a car.

"Our Buick store sells Buicks like crazy," Waybright says. "A Lucerne has a 150 market days supply metric. In the past, I would hesitate to buy that car and, in some cases, I wouldn't do it because I was targeting a 70-to-80-day market days supply. But now I may buy that car if I have the metrics to prove it will sell and the vehicle has the right equipment. We have accepted the fact that it's okay to buy that car as long as it's bought properly."

Taken together, the centralized buying team now purchases between 40 percent and 45 percent of the dealer group's inventory every month. The tally blends online and physical auction purchases and varies based on the volume of trade-ins and new vehicle sales at Kelley stores. (For trade-ins and appraisals, Waybright works with sales managers at each dealership to ensure they're "on the money.")

"I track everything," he says. "Our buyer recap shows each buyer's hours per purchase (target = 2.5 hours), average cost, average cost to market, average odometer and average market days supply. We do this for appraisers in each store, too."

I asked Waybright whether he offers his buying team any pay plan incentives for hitting the strategic marks and helping drive the dealer group's overall inventory turn and ROI.

"We do," he says. "We pay a small bonus based on the front end gross of all the purchased units. We track the retail deals and wholesale losses. It might be between $500 and $700 in additional income, depending on the month. It helps make sure everyone's working together."

A positive consequence of this buyer bonus plan: They have a vested stake in the vehicles and, if they're discounted at retail and grosses diminish, "they're on the phone to find out what happened," Waybright says.

Centralized, metrics-based pricing: During the early stage of his ROI-focused reinvention efforts, dealer Tom Kelley allowed managers in individual stores to set the prices for their used vehicles for the first 15 days. This practice has since shifted to a centralized approach to pricing under Waybright's direction to ensure vehicle prices reflect market realities, rather than a manager's intuition.

"There's no emotion in our pricing," Waybright says. "Typically, we're 97 percent to 98 percent price to market out of the gate. We'll drop the prices as the vehicles age, sometimes down to 87 percent."

He has designated an administrative assistant to handle the initial pricing and re-pricing of used vehicles, whether they come from auctions or trades.

"Loraine is very analytical," Waybright says. "Our pricing and re-pricing is strictly based on the metrics and targets we've set up. If she has questions, or there's a discrepancy, she'll get me involved. There are cases where we have a 25-day-old car and the market shifted, or a car where we've put too much into reconditioning and I have to drop it $1,000 to get it back on target.

"Loraine's leeway gets extended as the car ages on us. She knows our goal at 45 days is to get that thing out of here ASAP."

When the pricing changes are complete, they're sent to Waybright, as well as the managers and porters in each dealership.

"Everyone knows the new price and, if there's a question or a deal underway, they just call," he says.

Administrative help for vehicle logistics: In addition to pricing vehicles, Waybright relies on a second administrative assistant to serve as a "transport specialist" who coordinates the movement of cars the buying team has purchased at auctions.

In addition, the specialist manages transports of the handful of cars that the Kelley stores send to auction. Those cars, Waybright notes, have dwindled in number in recent years, from about 100 a month to less than 10 per month. "We had a good relationship with the auctions. They hate us now. We're retailing those cars we used to ship away," he says.

Waybright says the administrative help is critical to ensure the buying team focuses its efforts on finding and acquiring the "right" cars, rather than worrying about details of getting cars to/from the dealerships.

A related point: The group's main buyer handles arbitrations on auction-purchased used vehicles that do not match up with the condition, mileage or other factors the buyers evaluated as they acquired a car.

Information transparency: Every Monday morning, Waybright and his buyers go to a Kelley dealership to meet with managers. The rotating meetings help Waybright keep attuned to the inventory needs at each store.

During the meetings, Waybright and his buyers review each dealership's inventory against the strategic performance metrics and review plans for the cars they intend to purchase, re-price and wholesale.

The meetings have helped temper some of the inevitable concerns that arise among managers at different stores—Why did you buy this vehicle for them rather than us? Why did you wholesale our vehicle and not the one at the other store?

"Those questions used to happen over and over," Waybright says. "But we've made this completely transparent. If I provide the documentation for why we made a decision, they're more likely to under-stand and accept it. Because we track everything, they know we may understand their inventory needs better than they do.

"They also know we're doing what we do for the best interest of the company. We've proven our-selves and they don't get upset with us."

As my visit with Waybright ends, there's no mystery why dealer Tom Kelley put this former new car salesman, dealership general manager and 2008 NADA Dealer Academy graduate in charge of taking his ROI-focused reinvention in used vehicles to the next level.

It's clearly evident that Waybright has an aptitude for data and metrics. He tracks virtually every person and process that touches a used vehicle. He's mastered the science of blending metrics and metal.

What's more, Waybright's positive, can-do personality is a perfect fit for the coaching (and occasional cajoling) that's necessary to achieve buy-in and collaboration at each of Kelley's six dealerships.

"I'm very good at producing a very black and white picture with data," Waybright says. "I don't use my gut instinct or emotion in any of my decisions."

In some ways, Waybright is like a band leader who ensures each band member does his best to make sure the group sounds good as a whole. He's the helping hand behind the harmony at Kelley's dealerships.

"The neatest thing for us these past two years is the movement toward an overall successful outcome," he says. "It's not so much individual ideas and selfish motivations behind decisions."

REINVENTION ROADBLOCK:
THE USED CAR SHORTAGE

It's not uncommon for dealers to say their inventories suffer because of a "shortage of used cars."

I'd like to make the case that this is a misconception. The problem isn't a "shortage of used cars."

The problem is that dealers are unaccustomed to competing efficiently and effectively in what has become a far more competitive and challenging wholesale marketplace. They're struggling to figure out *how* to acquire the "right" cars when the auction lanes are choked with buyers, and everyone has eyes on the same cars.

For these dealers, a "shortage of used cars" often becomes the go-to excuse for a used vehicle department that isn't achieving its goals for inventory turn and return on investment (ROI). It often boils down to difficulties finding and acquiring the "right" cars, and it becomes a roadblock to reinvention.

Now, let's be clear: I'm not saying there isn't a shortening of the available supply of used vehicles, especially in some of the five-year-old and under segments. Overall, however, there are roughly 40 million used vehicles sold in the United States in any given year. This volume does not, at least to me, suggest a true-blue "used vehicle shortage."

Instead, it's simply a different market, one that requires dealers to apply more ROI-focused diligence and persistence to find and acquire the "right" used vehicle inventory. In short, it's harder out there to do a good job.

The following are four operational mantras for this new market. I've gleaned them from velocity dealers who have hit this roadblock to reinvention, and found a way through.

1. **Trade-ins are king. Period.** I propose the following benchmark for every dealer: Trade-ins should account for at least 45 percent of your used vehicle inventory, provided they are "on the money" and the "right" vehicles for your dealership.

I recognize this benchmark is more difficult
for some dealers to achieve than others. Some
franchises draw more customers than others.
However, the specific benchmark is less important than the intended outcome—relying less
on auctions to acquire cars. (By my tally, most
auction purchases saddle each used car with an
additional $700 in costs for auction fees and
transportation.)

A growing number of velocity dealers are
doubling-down on efforts to acquire vehicles
through non-auction sources, whether it's off-
the-street, in the service lane, or via trades. In
addition, they are using available technology
and tools from AutoTrader.com, Kelley Blue
Book, Black Book and others to guide customers
through the trade-in appraisal process. Typically, this adds credibility and transparency to a
dealer's appraisal offer.

This emphasis on trade-in vehicles requires
additional management diligence and discipline.
Every appraiser must be held accountable for
the ROI of the vehicles they acquire. It's a fool's
game to simply say "let's get more trades" without ensuring every car meets the dealership's
used vehicle investment and profitability objectives (see box, next page).

2. Tried-and-true sources won't cut it anymore.
Given that the pipeline of late model cars
has been constrained in recent years, there's

Appraiser Evaluation Metrics

The following benchmarks reflect the performance of appraisers at top-tier velocity dealerships in the United States:

Look-to-book Ratio: 45 percent

Acquisition Cost to Market*: 80 percent

Reconditioning Estimate Accuracy: 10 percent or fewer estimates exceed actual repair order (RO) amounts.

* The Acquisition Cost to Market measures the ratio between the vehicle's acquisition cost and its average retail asking price.

a better-than-fair chance that weekly runs to nearby auctions won't supply a sufficient number of the "right" cars for a dealership.

Trent Waybright, director of used vehicle operations at Kelley Automotive, Fort Wayne, Ind., notes that he and a buyer recently went to the Indianapolis auction with a 55-unit buy list. They came home with five cars, a roughly 10 percent close ratio. Just two years ago, they would have easily purchased 20 or more cars.

"It's horrible," Waybright says. "But we still go because we'll typically find cars that weren't on the initial run list. Of those five cars, most were fresh cars that came into the auction. They're dealer cars that aren't pre-registered. Nobody had a heads-up on them and it's less likely there will be a bunch of bidders. We'll appraise them by phone."

Dealer Bill Pearson, formerly of Finish Line Ford, Peoria, Ill., notes he's recently begun scouring large, independent auctions in the Southeast to find the cars he needs for his dealership.

"The business isn't as easy as it used to be," Pearson says. "Maybe you don't have what you want to see in your backyard, but at the end of the day, you just have to go further to find the cars."

Note: In the next chapter, we'll discuss how dealers are using online auctions as an efficient way to expand a store's acquisition scope beyond regional wholesale outlets.

3. **"Short" deals are part of the game.** Velocity dealers have recognized that today's hot wholesale market translates to higher acquisition costs for some used vehicles. To address this, they approach these cars with a short-term mentality—buy the car, carefully manage reconditioning costs and sell it quickly.

From an investment perspective, this is similar to investing in a "short-term investment fund."[4] To be sure, it's not an optimal position.

---

[4] http://en.wikipedia.org/wiki/Short-term_investment_fund

However, in today's market, it's sometimes necessary to take these "short deals" to keep a store's "wheel of fortune" and ROI turning. I would add these "short deals" are far better for a dealership than buyers consistently coming home empty-handed because of a "used vehicle shortage."

4. **Technology-aided sourcing is a must.** One thing about auctions hasn't changed. They still fuel a buyer's pride and thirst to buy a car, just like they've always done. Successful velocity dealers note today's inventory management technology and tools help mitigate the emotions that can kill ROI-focused discipline in the lanes.

First, the tools provide market-focused buy lists that ensure buyers focus on the "right" cars for the "right" money. vAuto's Provision® system, for example, provides inventory recommendations that erase a buyer's tendency to "go with what they know" if the market instructs otherwise. In this way, the tools help dealers and buyers to go "wide and deep" as they source used cars.

Similarly, Provision provides vehicle-specific bid guidance to stop buyers from raising their hand when a car's acquisition price wipes out its ROI potential.

"There are plenty of cars out there to buy," says Jack Anderson, director of used vehicle operations for West Herr Automotive, Buffalo, N.Y. "But to find the black one with heated seats with low miles at the right price? That's a different story. "

Second, the tools allow for quick, on-the-spot appraisals that are sometimes necessary to assess the last-minute cars that may match a buy list recommendation but appear at the auction too late for any advance homework.

Third, the tools pinpoint the auctions where buyers are most likely to be successful. It's nearly impossible in today's wholesale environment to buy more than a handful of the "right" cars at the "right" price at any given auction. Today's inventory management tools help dealers map their acquisitions across multiple locations and send buyers to specific auctions and lanes to maximize their efficiency and effectiveness.

As velocity dealers acknowledge the realities of today's wholesale marketplace, they recognize that any struggle to acquire used vehicle inventory is less about the market, and a "used vehicle shortage," than their own efforts to effectively and efficiently adapt to this more challenging acquisition environment.

THE OTHER EVENING I WAS HAVING DINNER WITH DEALER MIKE SHAW OF MIKE SHAW AUTOMOTIVE GROUP, DENVER. I BROUGHT UP THE USED CAR SHORTAGE AND ITS effects for some dealers. He held up his hand. "A used car shortage? That's bullsh**. Dealers need to go get it done and turn their inventory in 25 days. With a fast turn, you fix all the problems caused by high gas prices and any so-called shortage of used cars."

Amen, Mike. Sometimes the old car dog has to nip a few heels to make a point.

REINVENTION ROADBLOCK:
THE NEED TO TOUCH
EVERY USED CAR

John Worthington hasn't been to an auction to buy used vehicles since May 2005.

It's not because he's stopped buying cars. In fact, he and his team at Doug Henry Automotive, Tarboro, N.C., work the auctions every day to buy used vehicles. They just don't go in person anymore.

"I've just found that the time away from the store is counter-productive," says Worthington, who serves as the Internet Sales Director and General Sales Manager for the five-store group's Chevrolet store. "I also believe we have more protection buying online."

Worthington's team sources about half of its 120-unit inventory via online auctions. And get this: He uses proxy bids to purchase every one of the roughly 20 units he and his team acquire each week. Worthington considers physical and simulcast auctions a less efficient and consequently less effective means of getting cars in today's market.

"We've been proxy bidding for a lot of years," he says. "I used to do a lot of Simulcast and a lot of SmartAuction. But I have more confidence with proxy bids because we're either going to get the car, or we're not."

Allow me to make a quick prediction: In five years, Worthington's proxy-bid only approach to acquiring used cars will become a recognized best practice for dealers who want to maximize their return on investment (ROI) in used vehicles. I make this prediction for four key reasons:

1. **The transition is beginning.** Manheim stats show only one in five dealers who participate in its online auctions use proxy bids. However, the number of vehicles that dealers "win" via proxy bids has doubled between 2011 and early 2012, from 5 percent to 10 percent of the total.

   "The data suggests dealers who use proxy bids are getting better at it," says Joe George, senior vice president for Manheim. "We fully expect to see this trend continue as we improve the online bidding platforms and more dealers see value in acquiring cars online."

2. **Online bidding processes will improve.** Remember the days when none of us felt comfortable buying anything online with a credit card? Those are largely gone as online retailers actively address consumer fears about transaction security and satisfaction with purchases. Even I've come around: Not long ago, I wouldn't buy a pair of shoes without first trying them on. Now, I'm comfortable with shoes purchased online because most retailers make it easy to return them if they don't feel, look or fit right.

This same dynamic is taking shape with online auctions and proxy bids. Adesa, Manheim and other auctions are working to ease dealer concerns about buying vehicles online. They're aware that the absence of condition reports on 50 percent or more of the available vehicles is a problem. They recognize they need to be proactive with dealers to demonstrate that processes for arbitration and vehicle returns pose less risk than they used to. They know they must provide a greater degree of transparency in the proxy bidding process itself, so dealers like Worthington get more than a "you were outbid" message when a proxy bid doesn't win a car.

The time required for these improvements is one reason why I've offered a conservative five-year window for my prediction. But make no mistake: This online marketplace will look a lot different in the months and years to come, and the dealers who embrace it first will have the advantage.

"I don't think we'd be where we are if we didn't take some risks," Worthington says. "It's like anything else. If you want to be successful at something, you have to roll up your sleeves and be willing to make mistakes. And when you make mistakes, you learn from them. If you're not willing to set yourself on that path and get started, it sets you that much further behind."

3. **Market realities will require it.** Worthington's decision to rely solely on proxy bids to acquire auction vehicles wasn't arbitrary. He weighed the value of being available to his sales team and customers in the dealership against what he and other dealers have found to be diminishing returns at physical auctions.

"The days of flying to an auction and getting a truckload of cars are long gone," says Jeff Lajoie, who manages used vehicle operations for Bertera Motors, Hartford, Conn. "You end up spending $200 to $300 more on each car to save $100 on freight. The value isn't there."

This reality is driven, in large part, by the increased demand among dealers for used vehicles and the shortening of supply as noted in the last chapter. This competitive environment is the "new norm."

For dealers who need auctions to supplement their vehicle acquisitions, this higher level of competition means it's necessary to cast a wider net to find and acquire cars in a more efficient and effective manner. Online auctions and proxy bids provide the most efficient means to expand the hunting grounds without leaving the dealership.

4. **The resistance will wear thin.** As I've discussed why dealers and managers choose not to use online auctions and proxy bids, I've found the reasons fall into two groups:

   1. *They believe they have to touch every vehicle before purchasing it.* I understand this thinking because it's intended to minimize the risks of acquiring a unit that doesn't live up to its condition report.

      But let's consider this approach from the perspective of lost opportunities: In the time it takes a used vehicle manager or buyer to travel to an auction and physically touch the cars on a buy list, guys like Worthington have already placed dozens of proxy bids for the cars they need and moved onto other tasks—perhaps closing a deal with a customer, appraising a trade-in or teaching a salesperson how to overcome an objection.

Likewise, Worthington says the risks of getting a clunker aren't as great as more traditional, "touch-the-car" dealers might believe. First, he doesn't bid on vehicles that lack condition reports or rank low, condition-wise, on auction rating scales. Second, he takes his right to arbitrate iffy purchases seriously. In fact, he tracks the rate of arbitration by specific auctions. If one becomes problematic, he takes his business to another. Finally, if a proxy bid-purchased car proffers a surprise when it arrives at his store, and he can't rectify it through arbitration, Worthington trusts the efficiencies and ROI-minded focus of his team to maximize the unit's profitability—and move on.

This is why I've come to recognize the "need to touch every car" is really a road-block to reinvention. It can slow acquisition effectiveness and the "wheel of fortune" at dealerships.

2. *They don't trust technology or lack the skills to use it effectively.* I often find this shortcoming lies under the surface at dealerships where buyers and managers believe it's necessary to "touch every car." In other

words, the need to "touch every car" is really a cover for an inability to embrace the technology and tools that can make used vehicle acquisitions more efficient and ROI-focused for a dealership.

I understand dealers may be loyal to long-time, less-tech-savvy buyers and managers. But the hand-writing is on the wall. These individuals will either need to bone up their skills, get help from someone else who is less technology-challenged or find another job in the dealership or elsewhere that is more forgiving of their lack of technical proficiency.

"I fought technology for the longest time," says dealer Mike Shaw of Mike Shaw Automotive, Denver. "I went to Greece for three weeks with a computer. I forced myself to learn it. I've got so much going on that I needed to leave the country to slow down and then speed up. I did this because I realized I was slowing the whole organization down."

THREE PROXY BID PLAYBOOK TIPS FROM VELOCITY DEALERS

The following tips come from velocity dealers who have reinvented their used vehicle acquisition

"I Get Jacked Too Often With Proxy Bids"

This comment comes from a dealer who doesn't trust online auction proxy bidding.

The distrust, which dealers often express, flows from a sense that auctions will "run up" bids on vehicles when online proxy bids are in play. In essence, the dealers say they rarely win cars for less than their maximum bid amounts.

I took this concern to top executives at Manheim. The goal: Get real data to prove or disprove this common perception among dealers.

I wasn't terribly surprised to find that the data paints a different picture of proxy bidding success than what dealers often believe.

For example, Manheim data shows that most proxy bids "win" cars for less than the maximum bid amounts. On Manheim Simulcast, proxy bids win vehicles at their maximum amounts only 19 percent of the time; on OVE, the ratio is 41 percent.

To me, the data suggests that dealer concerns about getting "jacked" using proxy bids are greatly exaggerated.

processes to acquire cars more efficiently and effectively using online auctions and proxy bids:

1. **Determine your risk threshold.** Both Worthington and LaJoie will not bid on vehicles that lack a condition report. Period. Similarly, they will only bid on cars that receive the highest condition ratings from auctions. Both recognize this bidding practice reduces the number of vehicles they'll consider. But it's a trade-off: Since they can't physically touch the cars, they need to minimize the risk of acquiring units that end up being more trouble than they're worth.

"If a car isn't as promised, I can arbitrate," LaJoie says.

2. **Bid to buy.** Some dealers say they purposely hedge their proxy bid amounts in an effort to "steal" a car or minimize the risk of acquiring too many vehicles at the same time. Neither approach is a winning strategy for effectively and efficiently acquiring vehicles with proxy bids.

"If you're going to pay a certain amount for the car live, why don't you bid for that amount?," asks Becky Kirby, chief financial officer for Edd Kirby's Adventure Chevrolet, Dalton, Ga. "You know the purchase price you can live with and what you have to do to acquire the car. Dealers have to do this if they want to win vehicles. The odds are that dealers are not going to get all their cars through proxy bidding."

Worthington agrees. A proxy bid for anything less than a competitive amount is a waste of time. To ensure he sets the "right" bid amounts, Worthington uses his inventory management system to appraise a car, factor in his expected reconditioning costs and retail asking price and determine the bid amount that works for the car and his ROI and profit objectives.

"We bid with about a $2,000 profit objective," he says. "We follow the numbers. If we win, we win. If we lose, we lose."

I checked with Manheim to see how this "bid to win" mentality might play out with proxy bids. I was surprised to find the following:

- **Losing proxy bids on Manheim Simulcast typically land 23 percent below the selling price of a vehicle.** If the average wholesale vehicle price is $14,000, the losing proxy bids were off by more than $3,200.

- **Losing proxy bids on OVE typically fall 5 percent below the selling price of a vehicle.** This translates to a $700 gap on a $14,000 unit.

These figures suggest that many dealers are hedging their proxy bids, rather than setting them with the intention of acquiring vehicles.

3. **Know your close ratio, and play to it.** Worthington averages a 10 percent close ratio on proxy bids.

If he needs 30 cars, he sets between 300 and 350 proxy bids at one or more auctions. He tracks his close ratios with a Google mail account—he simply tallies and compares the number of "outbid" messages to his proxy total.

I asked Worthington if he's concerned that as he sets his maximum bid amounts he'll win too many cars.

"Normally, the auctions run the higher volume cars in batches," Worthington says. "You'll have 15 PT Cruisers in a row, 15 Impalas and 15 Malibus. In each block, we would only make three or four bids. Then, we'll skip a block and make other bids. If we get the four cars we need, we can then log into the auction and zero out the rest of the proxy bids available for that model.

"We have four or five people who receive the confirmation e-mails when we win a car. We're all in the store and we all know we have bids out there. It's just building a process around whatever you want to avoid."

A-ha! Worthington's process makes the commonly held fear of winning too many cars among dealers a non-issue.

A related benchmark: Manheim reports that dealer's proxy bids typically win vehicles about 7 percent of the time on its Simulcast auction and 20 percent of the time on OVE. The latter stat owes partly to OVE's auction-style bidding platform; dealers are not competing with live bidders in a physical auction lane.

I've focused this chapter on online auctions and proxy bidding because I believe they represent the "last mile" for ROI- and reinvention-minded dealers who want to acquire used vehicles in the most cost- and time-efficient manner possible.

I recognize that many dealers are currently uncomfortable using these online venues to feed their used vehicle inventories. However, I believe these wholesale purchasing platforms will soon become the norm for dealers who seek to maximize their used vehicle investments and profitability.

As the old saying goes, it's the early bird that gets the worm.

REINVENTION IN ACTION: CONTROLLING ACQUISITION COSTS TO BOOST ROI

Cary Donovan gets a lot of phone calls from dealers.

The dealers are seeking Donovan's diagnoses for problems in used vehicle inventory management. Typically, the calls relate to one of two scenarios:

1. **The dealers can't seem to eliminate inventory age issues.** Despite their best efforts to buy the "right" cars and price them competitively, they still have too many units that hit the 45-day or 60-day limit. The dealers ask Donovan for guidance to retail these cars more quickly to maximize their return on investment (ROI) potential.

2. The dealers want to increase their sales volumes.
Many of Donovan's callers have adopted velocity principles for their used vehicle inventories, and increased sales volumes by double-digit percentages. Now, however, they want to move the needle again to increase the velocity of their dealership's "wheel of fortune."

Donovan gets these calls given the reputation he and his employer, the Sam Swope Auto Group, Louisville, Ky., have garnered as one of the top-performing dealer groups in the country when it comes to used vehicles. As vice president and director of used vehicle operations for Swope's 15 stores, Donovan has led an impressive reinvention effort that consistently delivers 1,000 used vehicle sales each month and turns the group's inventory 20-plus times a year.

Donovan says both issues the dealers raise relate to the way they regard the ROI potential for their used vehicles as they acquire them. Yes, it goes back to the old saying "you make your money when you buy the car."

"Nine times out of 10 I'll see the same things as I look at these dealers' inventory metrics," Donovan says. "I'm looking at the blend of their inventory and their average investment cost per unit. At most dealerships I review, the average investment cost is too high.

"At my dealerships, our most expensive cars are the ones that get old the quickest," he says. "I've found that the more I compress average investment cost, the volumes are higher, and the grosses and inventory turn are better."

Donovan aims for an average investment cost below $15,000—a benchmark that is not easy to achieve given the high-line stores in the Swope family and the competitive pressures to acquire used vehicles. As he reviews other dealer inventories, the figure is often well north of $16,000.

"A lot of time you think the higher investment cost of unit, the higher the return on investment should be," he says. "Theoretically that should be true but it doesn't always run that way, especially as the more expensive units age."

Used vehicle consultant Tommy Gibbs of Tommy Gibbs and Associates, Treasure Island, Fl., affirms Donovan's assessment that the average investment cost of inventory is often a problem for dealers.

"The more dealers can keep the average cost down, and ensure the faster turn on expensive cars, the more money they'll be making," Gibbs says. "It's funny. Everybody knows this to be true. When I present this to dealers, it's like someone hits them on the head with a two-by-four. They'll say, 'That makes sense. Why do I have all these $30,000 cars in my inventory?'"

Donovan requires each store to send a daily report that compares the average inventory investment cost to the prior day and shows the variance. "I'm not looking for a specific amount, I just want it to be lower than yesterday," he says. "They don't like when the report shows they are up $480 because they bought a $60,000 Mercedes on a trade. It's not a beat-up tool."

The report doesn't just go to Donovan. Everyone who touches a used vehicle, from buyers to fixed operations to detailing to the lot managers, sees the daily number. "Everybody understands that our objective is to drive the average cost of the investment down," Donovan says. "If everyone's looking at this number, great things happen."

Donovan and Gibbs shared three prescriptions to help dealers manage their average inventory investments to minimize age and volume issues:

- **Be wary of too many "easy" auction acquisitions.** Donovan notes that his evaluation of a dealer's used vehicle inventory often reveals a reliance on program and fleet cars from auctions. These are "safe" cars to many dealers because factory warranties help cover reconditioning risks.

  These cars are "easy to buy but they're not a 'steal' the way they were in 2008-2009," he says.

The higher-dollar cars pose a problem for inventory turns and ROI because they often compete price-wise with new vehicles and, in some markets, there are fewer customers with the economic means to buy these cars.

"The salesman will always take the route of least resistance. If he can put someone in a new car for the about the same money, what will he do? He'll put him in the new car," Gibbs says. "He's got more options for financing and other factors."

To address this, Donovan's team has doubled-down on its efforts to acquire vehicles via trade-ins, service lanes and off-the-street purchases. The goal is to find cars for less money and maintain the average inventory cost benchmark.

- **Monitor and manage your costly cars.** Even with a goal to maintain a low average inventory investment, dealers should not shy away from more expensive cars if they offer a retailing and ROI opportunity. The key is to manage these cars in a way that assures they move quickly.

In his daily reports, Donovan also includes a run-down of the top 10 most expensive units in each store's inventory. The goal is to highlight the vehicles that pose the greatest ROI and inventory turn rate risks, and prompt pricing and merchandising decisions to help retail the vehicles more quickly.

Gibbs recommends that dealers price all of their top 10 most expensive vehicles below a 100 percent price to market metric to "make them go away." He offers one exception to this ROI-focused rule: Cars that are always good money-makers for a dealership don't always need to be on the list.

"Otherwise, dealers need to make sure those cars are priced to ensure someone can come in and buy it from you today," Gibbs says.

- **Understand how a unit's cost and inventory age affect ROI.** The rule to remember is this: ROI sags faster on higher-cost used vehicles as they age compared to lower-cost units. Gibbs offers the following example:

A dealer makes $2,500 on a $12,000 car after 25 days in inventory. The ROI is 303 percent. At 60 days, the ROI drops to 141 percent.

The same dealer makes $2,500 on a $27,500 car after 27 days in inventory.

The ROI is 131 percent. At 60 days, the
ROI drops to 61 percent.

"There are two things that hurt the
$27,500 car," Gibbs says. "I had too much
money in it, and I kept it for 60 days. Even
if I grossed $2,500 at 60 days, which
rarely happens, I really didn't make any
money on it."

REINVENTION ROADBLOCK: THE "EXTRA MILE" IN RECONDITIONING

Every afternoon, the "bullpen" meets at the Bill Marsh Auto Group, Traverse City, Mich.

The meeting typically includes Tedd Pless, general sales manager; Justin Jorkasky, inventory manager; a body shop or reconditioning center foreman and sales managers from each of the group's dealerships.

The "bullpen" gathers to examine every car the dealer group has acquired on a trade-in. They're here to make the call whether a car has a future at one of the five Marsh stores, or it's headed for wholesale.

"We line everything up," Pless says. "We discuss what we should be repairing on the car, how close the appraiser came to the actual reconditioning estimates and how we should price the car if we're going to retail it.

"If the appraiser estimates are off, it's a coaching opportunity," he says. "These guys want to know if they're good at what they do, and it's our job to tell them."

"We're making fewer mistakes on trade-ins since we started this," Jorkasky adds.

Such meetings are examples of the level of communication that today's used vehicle market now requires of variable and fixed operations managers and others who touch used vehicles during their dealership lifecycles. The discussions ensure everyone understands each vehicle's inherent opportunities and risks and the game plan for addressing them.

"Communication is critical," says dealer Mike Marsh. "You have to work out inefficiencies in appraisals, acquisitions and reconditioning. Our reconditioning touches every part of the company. You can't just do it department by department anymore."

For many dealerships, the type of collaboration the Marsh group employs to manage reconditioning costs does not occur. Instead, there is often a reflexive decision to acquire vehicles and "go the extra mile" to ready these cars for retail, irrespective of whether the additional repair/reconditioning costs effectively kill a unit's ROI and profitability potential.

In the past, these reflexive decisions were okay. Dealers could largely count on a return on their reconditioning investment. They could get away with charging retail rates or more for reconditioning work, because there was less pressure on front-end gross profit margins.

Today's environment, however, is less forgiving. It's now become necessary to determine the "right" amount of reconditioning for every vehicle and ensure these costs enhance rather than hurt the ROI and profitability potential in used vehicles.

For example, the Marsh "bullpen" recently reviewed a 2007 Sebring with 27,000 miles. They'd purchased the car cheap, in part due to some hail damage. Now, the "bullpen" faced the critical question: How much reconditioning work does this car need?

Jorkasky thought the car should get the paint job to earn gross in the body shop and fixed operations. Pless also saw the potential, but he didn't like the $2,000 estimate for reconditioning work.

Dealer Bill Marsh, who participates in the "bullpen" sessions when available, made the final call.

"We put out a good product here, but I saw this car as an opportunity," Marsh says. "It had very little hail damage. But there was a story there. We could show the KBB value and offer a 'hail damage' price. Customers could see why we priced the car cheap."

The team ran with Marsh's decision, and the vehicle sold for about $10,500, just as Marsh thought it would.

"That's the beauty of the roundtable discussion," Jorkasky says. "I had a different thought on the car."

"He's an optimist," Pless says. "I was thinking about an exit strategy. I didn't want to turn a $2,000 problem into a $4,000 problem."

This is the kind of reconditioning vigilance that is necessary to maximize ROI and profitability in used vehicles in today's market. The Marsh "bullpen" effectively guarantees that the reconditioning team won't "go the extra mile" unless a car warrants the top-notch treatment and its likely retail price point can support the additional cost.

In addition to "bullpen"-like discussions, velocity dealers are taking other steps to monitor reconditioning costs and maximize used vehicle ROI and profitability:

1. **Charge less than retail rates for reconditioning labor and parts.** I think the way dealers mark-up the labor and parts for reconditioning is a dead-end street. It's a practice that will, over

time, be out of step with today's more margin-compressed marketplace.

I'm not suggesting that dealers can't get a return on reconditioning work, provided it's called for on a vehicle. But I believe the "retail rate-or-better" philosophy has passed.

This is the "new normal" at some dealerships: Dealers must charge lower-than-retail rates for reconditioning parts and labor to reduce the costs it adds to vehicles. This operational change helps preserve the margin "spread" on every car, and can drive a dealer's ability to make more deals.

"I took my internal labor from $85 to $70 an hour, and I took down my parts mark-up from 45 percent to 25 percent," says Marc Ray, vice president and partner at Grogan's Towne Chrysler, Toledo. "I'm still making good money there.

"But I can buy a couple more cars a month, I believe, by having less expense in service. In the long run, that will create more business in the back-end because they're getting more volume."

This is how a growing number of velocity dealers are rethinking and reinventing their costs for reconditioning. They recognize that velocity principles in service are essential to maximizing velocity and profitability in used vehicle sales. Like Grogan, these dealers are "all in."

I should say, however, that I respect the position of dealers like Mike Shaw of Mike Shaw Automotive, Denver. He doesn't really want to hear my way of thinking when it comes to retail rates in reconditioning.

"I disagree with you, Dale," Shaw says. "We need to stay at retail rates for as long as we can. We're going to retain more gross in service than we do in sales. But you've got to make sure they're not 'putting you together' in the service department with your used cars."

Some dealers have found what might be described as a "medium point." They don't *always* charge the used vehicle department retail rates or more for reconditioning. You might say these dealers pick their spots.

"I give my used car department the same menu pricing as I do retail customers," says Adam Claiborne, GM at Fernandez Honda, San Antonio. "If I offer a tire rotation and balance at $49 for customers, it's the same for the used car department. The id

ea is to cut costs and make the cars more competitive."

Claiborne says this change has helped reduce average reconditioning costs by $250—a savings he believes feeds his margin "spread" and sales volumes. "If you do another 30 cars a month, service is still doing a lot better," he says.

2. Trim the scope of reconditioning when appropriate. At some dealerships, the "go the extra mile" philosophy has shifted to "do what's required to make a car safe and look nice."

In practical terms, this means re-thinking the point at which tires or brakes should be replaced, or windows and upholstery require repairs. Dealers can no longer simply approve this kind of cosmetic work to "go the extra mile." This is especially true if a car's ROI and profitability is questionable.

It pains me to say this, quite frankly. I was brought up to believe that dealers should "never apologize for anything on a used car."

In today's market, however, some dealers do not have the option to "go the extra mile" if they want to price their vehicles competitively and achieve their goals for ROI and profitability. These stores are up against operators like Car-Max, where the cost factors for reconditioning are less than most franchised dealerships.

A potential bright spot: Dealers who have eased up on cosmetic work say they get little push-back from customers. When customers push back, dealers have the opportunity to make a car "right," close a deal and seed a loyal customer.

3. **Use lower-cost replacement parts when appropriate.** As velocity dealers look to trim reconditioning expenses, many find cost savings from lower-cost, aftermarket replacement parts.

   "I don't like to put non-Honda parts on my used Honda inventory," Claiborne says. "But if it's a Chevy or another brand, we'll go to quality aftermarket parts to save money."

   Rich Ackman, a used vehicle consultant and former variable operations director for the Ohio-based Germain Group, says dealers who focus on sourcing lower-cost parts can shave up to $300 off the average cost to recondition cars.

   "You can buy a tire for $150 or $60," Ackman says. "When you start adding it all up, it becomes real money."

4. **Monitor reconditioning work and time on every vehicle.** At the Marsh Group, Jorkasky tracks every car through each stage of the dealer group's reconditioning process. He uses the same dry-erase boards my friend Russ Wallace used to ensure efficiency and speed for the work on every vehicle. The goal is a 48 hour turn-around, and many vehicles move through reconditioning in less time.

   This benchmark puts the Marsh team near the front of the line when it comes to reconditioning efficiency. The impressive throughput owes to coordinated and disciplined management, people and processes.

I recognize it's a struggle for many dealers to reduce reconditioning turn times to five or even three days on a consistent basis. But I believe achieving these benchmarks is a must to maximize used vehicle ROI and profitability in today's margin-compressed environment.

As the old saying goes, less is definitely more when it comes to the time it takes to recondition a vehicle.

"We have to become more efficient in what we do. Period," Marsh says. "That's no different in our business than any other business these days."

Next up: We'll take a closer look at how a Wisconsin dealer has reinvented his reconditioning processes and brings a tidy sum to his bottom line.

REINVENTION IN ACTION: FIXING CARS FOR SPEED, PROFITS

Dealer Keith Kocourek of Kocourek Chevrolet, Wausau, Wis., finally got tired of a see-saw effect in his dealerships.

He describes the ups-and-downs this way:

As he adopted velocity principles, he'd price his used cars to sell quickly. His goal was to improve the dealership's annual inventory turn rate and increase sales volumes.

'With our pricing, we'd immediately sell out of cars. Then, we'd go out and buy 30 cars and drop them in the service department," Kocourek says. "They couldn't get to them. We'd immediately burn 10 or

15 days to recondition the cars. In the meantime, our sales would go down because we didn't have the inventory. Then, as they trickled in, we'd have a glut of cars that were already 10 to 15 days old. You can't maintain a 28-day turn if you're burning 10 to 15 days in the shop.

"You have to take the buying, reconditioning and detailing process and spin it down to three, four or five days. That way if you have a big sales week, you can get more meat through the grinder. Out of the other end comes a car that's ready to be sold."

This realization led Kocourek to reinvent the way his dealerships handle the reconditioning of used vehicles. Like other dealers who have adopted velocity principles, Kocourek recognized that it's a significant challenge to change the culture of service and parts departments to treat reconditioning work with the same or higher priority as work from retail customers.

His fix: A centralized reconditioning and detailing center in a separate building that focuses all of its efforts on reconditioning used cars to ensure they're ready more quickly and offer the highest return on investment (ROI) and profitability potential.

"We've cut the through-put time by two-thirds," Kocourek says. "If I drop 25 cars in there on Thursday, I have every confidence that by Monday, those cars will be finished and on the lot. It's not just one, two or five cars. It's all of them.

"The technicians are all flat-rate. They're not working on new cars, and they're not out cutting grass. They are hungry. Their productivity went from 70 percent to 110 percent to 115 percent. They're working harder to get the cars through and out to the lot."

This operational reinvention has provided significant benefits for Kocourek's dealerships:

1. **Lower reconditioning costs.** Kocourek estimates his average $730 reconditioning cost is about $400 less than it used to be. This improvement, which helps protect his margin "spread" on every used car, flows from less overhead and personnel costs required to handle the reconditioning work at the separate facility.

   The facility cost runs about $20/foot compared to $100/foot for the service departments at his dealerships. Similarly, the technicians and detailers who work in the facility command lower hourly rates than those working in the dealership—although Kocourek's incentives for efficiency and speed mean some paychecks nearly match those of in-dealership technicians. The incentives are based on detailers and technicians consistently achieving productivity rates higher than 100 percent.

2. **Faster inventory turns, increased sales volume.**
   With less time required for vehicle reconditioning,
   Kocourek is now able to consistently maintain
   a 25-day supply of vehicles in his inventory and
   meet his goal to turn his inventory investment at
   least 15 times a year. His five-store dealer group
   is on track to sell 350 units per month.

   "The cars are getting done and on the lot faster,"
   Kocourek says. "We've gotten out of all those
   peaks and valleys where the sales flat-line. We're
   steadily increasing our volumes, and the sales
   people aren't wondering what cars they'll have
   to sell."

3. **Improved "wheel of fortune" profitability.** The
   centralized reconditioning facility has become its
   own profit center. Kocourek says it handles 250
   cars per month and averages a $380 gross per
   unit. "It's found money," he says.

   At the same time, the decision to centralize
   reconditioning helped Kocourek focus his dealership service and parts departments on increasing
   their customer pay work and retention.

   "The capacity in the service departments has now
   exploded," he says. "We've got room for another
   15 to 18 cars a day because we don't have the
   internal work. The shops have to market themselves and go after customer pay work, which
   has helped our retention rates skyrocket."

Of course, this "wheel of fortune" means a substantial increase in net profits for all dealership operations. Kocourek says that figure has increased 70 percent or more at his stores.

"Our competitors are scratching their heads and wondering what's next," he says. "They're wondering how we can sell a car for $300 less and make $200 more in profits. This is why we've been able to buy more stores. Our stores are record-profitable. If it didn't get any better, I'd be happy."

4. **A training ground for future talent.** Kocourek's centralized detailing and reconditioning center also serves as a proving ground for new employees. Several have moved on to positions as parts managers, service advisors and inventory acquisition specialists.

"It's a perfect opportunity to get someone in the door and see if they fit our culture," he says.

I've shared Kocourek's tale of reinvention because it highlights a logical way to eliminate the delays and inefficiencies that can undercut used vehicle ROI and profitability in fixed operations. It also details the scope of reinvention that sometimes must occur as traditional dealership processes fail to meet the needs of a velocity-driven business model for used vehicles.

Kocourek will be the first one to relay that the scale and scope of operational change he undertook requires courage, faith and fortitude.

"We went through a bunch of pain in our service and parts departments," Kocourek says. "But if I can standardize my used vehicle operations like a parts department or a service department, I can calculate gross profit before it happens. That's a predictable future."

REINVENTION ROADBLOCK:
PRICING FOR PROFITABILITY,
NOT PROFIT

In early 2009, Marc Ray recognized that his dealer-ship's used vehicle pricing was out of step with today's Internet buyers.

"I was like every other dealer," says Ray, vice president and partner at Grogan's Towne Chrysler, Toledo. "I was the guy who would take a car, mark it up $3,000, take it into service and get an $800 bill, and then mark it up another $800. No wonder I wasn't selling any cars."

Ray's recognition that a mark-up-from-cost approach to pricing used vehicles wasn't working came the hard way.

A year earlier, he'd invested all of his savings and staked his future as a partner in the Toledo dealership. It was a risky, life-defining moment for a college drop-out who'd toiled hard for 18 years in the business.

Then the bottom fell out in the summer of 2008. Car sales came to a standstill.

"We hit the wall," he says. "We had to drain our cash to stay in business. We were in bad shape."

He began a determined hunt to find a way to save his dealership and investment. Like other dealers, he turned to used vehicles to build back the cash flow his dealership required to survive.

"I had to figure something out with used cars," he says. "They're my cash. We needed to turn cars faster to make our payroll and pay our bills."

Ray's instincts told him he needed to get more eyeballs on his used vehicle inventory. He called his AutoTrader.com rep. The conversation led to a substantial increase in his spending for online vehicle listings.

"I took my AutoTrader.com budget from $5,000 to $16,000," he says. The additional expenditure spurred more sales and helped carry the dealership through December.

But it wasn't enough.

"We were spending all this money and we were still not doing the volume," Ray says.

In January of 2009, he started reading up on velocity principles for inventory management. It didn't take long for Ray to understand his $3,000-mark-up-from-cost approach to pricing was killing his turn potential with today's price-minded Internet buyers.

"That's when the switch flipped for me," he says. "I felt like an idiot."

Not long after this "a-ha!" moment, Ray pulled an all-nighter to update all the vehicle descriptions and prices for his used vehicles. He was determined to get rid of his older-age inventory and fill his lot and online listings with fresh, market-priced cars. Of course, he took some significant wholesale hits.

"I'll never forget," Ray says. "I was on vacation and my partner called and said, 'what the ****! are you doing? You're selling these cars and losing your ass.'

"There was one car in particular, a Sebring convertible. He'd put $7,000 too much in the car on trade and it had a problem in service. He said, 'you're losing $5,000 on this car.' I said, 'just because you overpaid doesn't mean somebody's going to come pay me for your mistake.'

"From then on, that's where things really started to take off for us," Ray says. "It was incremental. We finished our first month with 54 cars, then 75 and then 90. We're now averaging 140 a month."

Ray's experience reflects what many dealers have encountered as they've embraced velocity management principles and recognized that their asking prices for used vehicles must at least strike today's online buyers as "in the market" if not "on the money."

This is a difficult pill for many traditional dealers to swallow. For decades, dealers have "made the market" for used vehicle pricing. The traditional mark-'em-up-and-wait-for-a-buyer approach to used vehicle pricing has lined many dealer bank accounts with a sizable cash flow in the past.

The basic idea behind this traditional pricing approach is that a vehicle's price determines its gross profit potential. If a dealer wanted more gross profit, he'd simply raise the price. Buyers, meanwhile, were largely beholden to these pricing practices, unless and until they pushed back hard enough in negotiations to get a purchase price that came close to or matched the price for a similar car they'd seen at another dealership.

These days, however, the shoe is on the buyer's foot. The Internet has brought a greater degree of transparency to dealer pricing. Those who continue the standard, $3,000 to $4,000 mark-ups, will find themselves exactly where Ray landed in early

2009—sitting on an inventory with too many aging cars and too-few buyers.

The key to used vehicle pricing in this more information-efficient and price-transparent marketplace could be put into a simple, six-word mantra: Price cars for profitability, not profit.

This may seem counter-intuitive to some dealers, particularly those who've long-regarded their average front-end gross profit as the most critical benchmark for ROI and profitability in their used vehicle departments.

Perhaps the best way to explain the difference between pricing cars for profitability, not profit might be to think of the difference between contact hitters and sluggers in baseball.

Sluggers, as we all know, are the players most likely to aim for the fences on the first pitch and those that follow. They want the home run and often approach each swing with a trot around the bases in mind. Typically, a baseball team's top slugger will also have the one of the highest strike-out averages and lowest on-base percentages on a team.

This is the equivalent of dealers who aim for the "home run gross" through standard $3,000 to $4,000 mark-ups on every car. They're swinging for the fences and, just like sluggers in baseball, they'll likely strike out more often than send a ball to the bleachers.

Contact hitters, meanwhile, are more circumspect. They may aim for the fences on a first pitch, but only if the ball's in their sweet spot. More often, contact hitters adjust their swing to meet the pitch, whether it's a fastball, slider, sinker or curveball. They'll send the occasional ball into the stands, but it's more likely they'll consistently tick off singles and doubles, and help their team by getting on base and scoring a run. This more judicious use of their time at the plate typically translates to a higher batting average and on-base percentage than other players in the dugout.

In today's market, dealers need to be more like contact hitters than sluggers as they price their used vehicles. They need to view every car as a pitch and, like a contact hitter, adjust their swing (their pricing) to fit the pitch. Depending on the car, dealers might be able to set a price that's a home run.

More often, however, dealers will need to set prices that translate to singles, doubles and the occasional triple. Today's market is too efficient, competitive and margin-compressed to allow a home run on every car. In this environment, the "right" price for a car would reflect the current market *and* a dealer's goals for inventory turn rates and profitability.

But get this: Unlike the contact hitters in baseball, who can only guess at the kind of pitch they'll see at the plate, dealers have the ability to know the precise opportunity or risk each vehicle offers and set their prices accordingly. This pricing assessment requires two key steps:

Step 1: Understand the car's likely emotional appeal with buyers. Most dealers don't need any help with this. They have the discerning car "eye" to say, "Now, that's a car!" or "Well, I think we can do okay with this unit." This instinctive read can and should feed decisions on how to swing, or price, the vehicle for maximum profitability.

Step 2: Assess the car's value as an investment. This is a rare step for traditional dealers, and one that velocity dealers like Ray take on every vehicle. It requires reviewing each vehicle's market days supply and price to market metrics to determine the price that offers the best path to profitability on a unit. This equates to a contact hitter studying each pitch and adjusting his swing for a hit. The metrics, coupled with the assessment of the car's emotional appeal, leads to market-smart pricing decisions.

For example, if a vehicle has strong emotional appeal and its market days supply is low, the car may warrant a slugger-style first swing, or price, as it hits the front line. This is because the market days supply indicates there are fewer competing vehicles available. This car—call it a mint 2010 Camaro with 15,000 miles—would likely warrant a price above the market because of its condition and mileage compared to the competition. It could be a "home run car" if the price connects with customers and it sells quickly. If it doesn't, Ray and other velocity dealers would gradually lower the price to ensure profitability as it ages in inventory.

By contrast, a vehicle with less emotional appeal and a high market days supply would likely require a contact hitter-style initial swing, or price, as it hits the front line. This is because the market days supply indicates the car has more competition. This unit—call it a 2007 Malibu with 75,000 miles—would likely require a price at or below the market to increase its appeal with buyers, compared to competing vehicles. If the car doesn't sell quickly, Ray and other velocity dealers would aggressively lower the price as it ages to make a retail sale and preserve profitability.

The point here is that a vehicle's price cannot be driven solely by the front-end gross profit a dealer hopes to make with a customer. That's part of the picture, but more important is the relationship between the car's emotional appeal, condition, market competition and potential for profitability.

In other words, pricing used vehicles in today's market is not about swinging for the fence every time. It's far more nuanced, just like the decisions contact hitters apply at the plate—go for the home run if the ball looks right, but otherwise get on base and score a run.

I should add that the price to market and market days supply metrics are not the only indicators velocity dealers use as they "price for profitability, not profit." In addition, online merchandising metrics, such as the conversion rate from search results pages and vehicle detail pages (SRP/VDP) are also important. These provide real-time indicators of how well the initial pricing decisions hold up with online buyers. We'll discuss those in greater detail in an upcoming chapter.

In the meantime, let's take a closer look at how The Car Group, the Los Angeles-based dealership management company headed by top-selling dealer Dave Conant of Norm Reeves Honda fame, blends an "eye" for cars and market-based metrics to "price vehicles for profitability, not profit" across its nine stores.

Chad Lemieux, the corporate used car director for the group, explains the group's approach.

First, Lemieux segments his inventory into "buckets" that reflect the inventory age of vehicles. The buckets are 0-25 days, 26-40 days, and 40-55 days. "At 56 days, it's a mandatory wholesale," he says. At that point, the car has run its course and "the market has spoken" about its retail potential.

Second, Lemieux aims for less than a 90 percent cost to market metric as an aggregate for vehicles that enter the initial age "bucket." This is a more nuanced position than the 84 percent cost to market metric that many velocity dealers strive to achieve for fresh cars.

"We don't have a set metric because there are vehicles that can work outside the metrics," Lemieux explains. "I use an 80/20 rule. I want 80 percent of the cars to fit a defined structure and 20 percent that meet a sound market case but may exceed the normalized average.

"A 15,000-mile car in a market where its competing cars are at 60,000 miles might have a cost to market of 99 percent," he says. "It's still a desirable car that offers a solid case for a return on investment even though it's outside the norm. Averages are just that. They are groups of information together, but they don't necessarily express everything."

Third, Lemieux sets his price to market benchmarks to get more aggressive as vehicles age—a practice that seeks to preserve profitability and spur a sale. Typically, this means pricing vehicles in the first "bucket" at a 99 percent price to market metric; the range is 94 percent to 96 percent for the second "bucket," and 90 percent to 92 percent for the third "bucket."

In this way, Lemieux is applying the "price vehicles for profitability, not profit" mantra every day. The results of this disciplined, market-focused approach to pricing are impressive. The Car Group's monthly used vehicle sales have climbed from 600 to nearly 750 under Lemieux's leadership. He notes the group typically sells more than half of its used vehicles within 25 days, a key driver behind its ability to turn its inventory 20 times a year.

"Our defining goal is to sell the highest amount of inventory at its most profitable point in the first bucket," Lemieux says.

I also asked Lemieux how pay plans for used vehicle managers and sales teams reflect the "pricing for profitability, not profit" mantra. Sure enough, the group's bonus and pay plans reward the behaviors that a baseball manager wants to see from his contact hitters—don't aim for the fences, get on base and score runs.

"Predominately, I don't believe you bonus a guy for making $3,000 a copy," Lemieux says. "You bonus when he makes $300,000 in the department."

Other velocity dealers have also improved their used vehicle ROI and profitability as they've adopted the "price vehicles for profitability, not profit" mantra.

"We pay close attention to price," says dealer Woody Butts, Jr., of Woody Butts Chevrolet, Cochran, Ga. "We know we're going to make the most money in the first 20 to 21 days we own a car.

We price our cars to be in the top five in our market from the beginning to ensure they sell quickly."

This pricing philosophy has helped Butts quadruple his used vehicle sales volumes from 20 to 85 units per month. "It's all about maximizing our inventory turns and our return on investment," he says.

Some readers may be thinking one of two things as they digest the "pricing for profitability, not profit" concept:

> *"Gee, thanks, Dale. You've just made my job as a dealer a lot harder."*

Or,

> *"I don't buy this at all. This is just going to kill my front-end grosses."*

To the first group, the next chapters will be important. It begins an examination of how dealers can leverage "pricing for profitability, not profit" through the online marketing and merchandising of their used vehicles.

To the second group, I would respectfully suggest re-reading Chapter 4.

Reinvention Roadblock: The Business Case for Classified Sites

Every dealer would agree that even when you price a used vehicle correctly, it won't sell unless a customer has the opportunity to see it.

This universal-type truth has been with us since Henry Ford brought the automobile to the masses a century ago. It's the reason dealers put their stores in high-traffic locations and take special pride in their "front line," the highly visible row of cars they select and place to catch customer attention and spur walk-ins and test drives.

For dealers, the "front line" has gone digital in today's Internet-driven marketplace. To be sure, dealers still take great pride in the physical "front line," but most have recognized they need to pay equal, if not greater, attention to the way they position and present their vehicles online.

In this new Internet-driven environment, the car remains the star. As we noted in earlier chapters, the "right" car at the "right" price are two essential ingredients to maximize a dealer's return on investment (ROI) and profitability in used vehicles.

There are two additional elements to a dealer's online merchandising equation we haven't yet addressed—how the "right" place and "right" presentation online can either make or break a used vehicle's ability to capture a customer's interest and create a sale in the showroom.

In this chapter, we'll focus on what I believe is the single-best "right" place for dealers to showcase their used vehicle inventory beyond their own dealership websites—the online classified sites like AutoTrader.com and Cars.com. In upcoming chapters, we'll address the "right" presentation, or the "digital details," a dealer must address across all online platforms that carry their used vehicle inventories.

Before we begin, however, I should offer a caveat for the more cynical readers: Yes, my company, vAuto, has been acquired by AutoTrader.com. As a result, I do have a vested interest in the success of its online classified platform. That said, however, I've always believed AutoTrader.com and Cars.com are an essential part of the online merchandising mix for dealers and their used vehicles.

In fact, this belief is the foundation for a cardinal rule at vAuto: We will not sell our technology and tools to dealers who do not use one or both of these online classified sites to merchandise their used vehicle inventories. This dictate owes to the universal truth noted above—dealers cannot effectively and efficiently sell used vehicles, let alone see the "wheel of fortune" benefits velocity management principles can create, if their cars are not visible to online shoppers.

WHY ONLINE CLASSIFIEDS ATTRACT USED VEHICLE SHOPPERS

There are two key reasons sites like AutoTrader.com and Cars.com remain top, go-to destinations for consumers interested in buying used vehicles.

1. The Format: Some accounts trace the lineage of classified advertising to a Boston News-Letter effort in 1704 to encourage readers to list items they wanted to buy or sell[5]. Others credit stone-carved public notices recovered during excavations of Pompeii, the Italian city lost when

---

[5]   http://en.wikipedia.org/wiki/Short-term_investment_fund

Mount Vesuvius erupted in 79 AD, as the earliest form of the classified medium.[6]

The point is that classified advertising has been around a long time and it's a format today's consumers are accustomed to using, either online or offline, to find used cars, real estate, jobs, business opportunities, dating partners, etc.

In addition to being a familiar format, classified ads lend themselves to the psyche of used vehicle shoppers. That is, used vehicle shoppers often focus first on finding the car that fits their wants and needs. Classified ads offer a highly efficient, fast-scan format for consumers to review a lot of vehicles quickly as they narrow their interests to a specific car.

"When it comes to used vehicles, the car is the star," says Cars.com founder and president Mitch Golub. "A used vehicle is a very unique one-of-a-kind asset. On the new car side, where vehicles are more commoditized by make/model, a dealership's brand and reputation are bigger factors."

It shouldn't surprise anyone that AutoTrader.com and Cars.com both got their start as publishers of printed classified advertising. The forerunner for AutoTrader.com included a stable of successful printed Trader-branded magazines that offered dozens of pages of used vehicles for sale. The founders

---

[6] http://www.sooperarticles.com/internet-articles/internet-marketing-articles/brief-history-classified-ads-358424.html

of Cars.com came from the newspaper business, where classified advertising consistently drove the largest share of revenue and profits.

In short, the classified advertising format works for selling used cars. Back in my day as a dealer, our used car manager wasn't doing his job if our store didn't have its weekly run of classified used vehicle listings ready for the ad rep by Thursday afternoon.

2. The Firepower: No dealer would argue that AutoTrader.com and Cars.com are the "big dogs" when it comes to attracting car shoppers to classified listings. Depending on the market, one or both of the companies are well known given their respective efforts to brand themselves as the "go-to" source for online buyers to research and find the vehicles that fit their wants and needs.

AutoTrader.com and Cars.com are "household names. They advertise on the Superbowl and World Series," says Shaun Kniffin, director of e-business development for Germain Motor Company, Columbus, Ohio. "Just looking at the amount of traffic we generate with Trader and Cars, from phone calls, e-mails, live chat and floor traffic, they're great places for our inventory."

"These companies spend millions to brand themselves," says Jason Ezell, president of Dataium, LLC, a Nashville-based company that tracks online vehicle shopping trends. He notes Auto-Trader.com, Cars.com and eBay are the three largest aggregators of vehicle shoppers. "Dealers need to put their cars and their money where the shoppers go."

WHY DEALERS DITCH CLASSIFIED SITES —AND COME BACK

It's not uncommon for dealers to get frustrated with online classified sites—and AutoTrader.com likely gets more heat from dealers than Cars.com.

This happened at Wyler Automotive, Cincinnati, as e-commerce director Kevin Frye was evaluating his third-party vendors amid efforts to cut costs in late 2008 and early 2009.

The group opted to pull the plug on its AutoTrader.com spending after analyzing the costs per lead and costs per sale. "We got out," says Frye. "We weren't seeing the return. The cost wasn't worth it."

Today, however, AutoTrader.com is part of the online merchandising mix for Wyler—a reversal of the earlier decision that owes to a better understanding of how today's online shoppers use classified sites like AutoTrader.com and the role they play in driving customers to the dealer's websites and its showroom floors.

The decision to re-up with AutoTrader.com followed a group-wide effort to put a greater focus on capturing and converting customers who visited the Wyler dealership websites.

"Without question, your No. 1 source of shoppers when it comes to e-commerce is going to be people searching for your name and going to your web-site," Frye says. "This should tell you that your No. 1 focus should be on your own website, converting shoppers into e-mails, phone calls and on-site visits.

"Before I throw a whole bunch of money out to other sites, I want to fish in my own pond and make sure I'm treating these people that have already searched for me by name with the best experience," he says.

This mindset led to the addition of technology and tools on the dealership's websites to provide online shoppers resources they want and would go else-where to get if they couldn't find them on a Wyler site. These include tools to handle online finance applications, trade-in evaluations and credit score estimators.

In addition, Frye focused on the inventory itself. "If I'm doing a poor job with photos or descriptions, of course I'm not going to get a good return on investment with AutoTrader.com or Cars.com or any of these other guys," he says.

The final leg of Frye's capture-and-convert effort came in the Wyler showrooms. The group rolled out a standardized customer relationship management (CRM) system to capture and source all customers—whether they came from dealership or third-party sites, sent an e-mail, called a number listed on other online sources or just walked in.

"The CRM sources customers correctly," Frye says. "Salespeople don't do this and they never will."

"Now that we can source things better, we're seeing a lot of our return with AutoTrader.com," he says. "I put much of our lack of previous performance on ourselves. Perhaps we weren't doing the best with photos or descriptions."

Dataium's Ezell says Frye's experience is similar to what he sees at dealer groups where Dataium's been hired to fully track the comings-and-goings of online vehicle shoppers.

Sixty to 70 percent of the traffic to most dealership websites flows from Google searches and, of those shoppers, roughly 40 percent dial up a dealership after scouting its vehicles on AutoTrader.com, Ezell says. The combined throughput of vehicle shoppers to dealer websites from AutoTrader.com and KBB.com translates to more than 50 percent of the total visits to dealer sites, according to AutoTrader.com data.

Ezell shares two key reasons for this overlap:

1. **Size and scope of classified sites.** AutoTrader.com and Cars.com have the most cars for consumers to shop, and they've been able to brand

themselves as easy-to-use, go-to destinations. The companies came of age as dealers debated the merits of putting inventory, let alone vehicle prices, online. As a result, the classified sites became and remain the best sources for vehicle shoppers to efficiently research a lot of different vehicles and to determine the vehicle they want to purchase. This is a key reason why consumers spend significantly more time on third party sites than either factory or dealer websites, industry stats show.

2. **The "path of least resistance."** "Consumers are less likely to submit a lead on a third-party site today than they used to be," Ezell says. That's because dealers have historically either failed to respond to leads (e.g., "cherry-picking") or shoppers have been inundated with follow-up calls as their initial e-mail got re-sold to multiple dealers.

Today, a majority of online shoppers take the "path of least resistance" and Google the dealership to see if the vehicle they spotted on AutoTrader.com is still available. If it is, the shopper is more likely to simply show up and look at the car rather than e-mail or call.

(**Note:** AutoTrader.com's customer sourcing studies show 64 percent of vehicle buyers say their first contact with a dealership came when they "walked in" the showroom. Similarly, company analytics show only 3 percent of vehicle shoppers who drill into a car's vehicle details page (VDP), will submit an e-mail. On Cars.com, only 7 percent of visitors e-mail, call or initiate a chat session with dealerships directly, Golub says. The company's also seeing shopper behavior evolve with growing mobile usage.

"Consumers doing research on their smartphone may look for directions or a map," he says. "Measuring mobile activity can provide great insight into walk-in traffic.")

"The indirect effect of AutoTrader.com or Cars.com is 10 to 15 times larger than the traffic dealers can measure themselves by counting leads," Ezell says. "I try to educate dealers that they should stop measuring the success of automotive portals on direct leads. That's the smallest number of the whole equation.

"You're going to lose 40 percent of your website traffic and lose several hundred phone calls if you cancel AutoTrader," he says. "When dealers do that, they often realize what they've lost."

Dana Pratt, e-business director for the Bill Marsh Automotive Group, Traverse City, Mich., says the group has found it's better to keep classified sites as part of its online merchandising mix rather than eliminate them. In spring 2011, the group stopped listing on AutoTrader.com for a few weeks.

"We didn't see any appreciable difference here in the business development center," Pratt says. "But our sales managers told us we needed to get back on

AutoTrader because our foot traffic in the show-rooms went down. We came back the next month."

Kniffin says he understands why some dealers would bristle at the costs they pay for putting their inventory on classified sites. But he believes they are an essential part of any dealership's online used vehicle merchandising matrix.

"With all of the phone calls, e-mails, live chats and clicks to our inventory that are happening, I can't imagine this would be considered a bad spend," Kniffin says. "Some people say they want to do it themselves, and I ask, 'why?' You fish where the fish are at, right?"

In the next two chapters, we'll dig into how dealers deploy what I call "advanced pixel proficiency" to ensure the "right" place and "right" presentation for used vehicles to maximize ROI, efficiencies and sales from their online merchandising efforts.

REINVENTION IN ACTION:
ADVANCED "PIXEL PROFICIENCY"

"It's a hell of a lot of work."

That's the consistent theme from velocity dealers when we discuss all the to-dos required to properly prepare and place used vehicle listings on dealership and third-party sites.

I totally get it. In my day as a dealer, we only took pictures of the cars we knew would be eye-grabbers—and typically did so only if we had a newspaper display ad slated for the week.

Now, dealers are hiring photographers and digital content analysts. They're building photo booths and quick-turn detailing and reconditioning centers. They start their days reviewing vehicle details page

(VDP) tallies on their used vehicles *before* they check the up log or walk the lot.

It's a decidedly different world out there for used vehicle retailers—one filled with what might be called a ton of "digital details" that often tests the technical skills and temerity of more traditional dealers and used vehicle managers.

My goal for this chapter on "advanced pixel proficiency"[7] is to offer some guiding metrics and principles to help dealers become more adept at managing the "right" presentation for merchandising their used vehicles on classified sites like AutoTrader.com and Cars.com to maximize their appeal with today's online shoppers. As noted in the last chapter, I believe these sites are the two most important "right" places for dealers to drum up buyer interest online. In the next chapter, we'll examine online marketing and merchandising best practices for other "right" places that should be part of a dealer's digital game plan.

Before we dive in, though, I need to make sure one thing is patently clear to dealers: When it comes to merchandising used vehicles on online classified sites, the bulk of the burden for success rests on your shoulders. It's not enough to sign up for AutoTrader.com and Cars.com, send them a check and expect results.

---

[7] "Pixel Proficiency" is a term introduced in my second book, Velocity 2.0: Paint, Pixels and Profitability. It refers to the digital elements required for presenting vehicles in a compelling fashion online.

If you don't have the "right" cars at the "right" price, you're toast. If you don't have the "right" presentation dialed in for every car, you've undercut each unit's potential appeal with online buyers. If you aren't actively managing your online merchandising metrics, your dealership and your vehicles aren't really in the game in today's Internet-driven environment.

To be sure, AutoTrader.com and Cars.com also have a stake in a dealership's online merchandising success. But their job is largely limited to two factors:

First, it's their responsibility to attract used vehicle shoppers to their respective platforms. Dealers should know the number of active shoppers in their market for each classified site. This tally is critically important as it helps dealers define their expectations for sales volumes and the geographic market areas that will help them achieve their sales goals.

For example, dealer Bill Pearson, formerly of Finish Line Ford in Peoria, Ill., previously dialed his AutoTrader.com merchandising package to draw shoppers from a 150-mile radius from the dealership. Now, the radius is more like 75 miles—a change he attributes to rising competition from other dealers to market and sell used vehicles.

"My competitive footprint is completely different than it was four years ago," Pearson says. "Back then, I could run over dealers near and far. Now the footprint is 75 miles, which means I'm competing with the same guys I compete with for new car sales."

Dealers should also recognize that the number of active shoppers varies between classified sites and individual markets, and it fluctuates due to economic trends and seasonality. In general, dealers should at least be aware of the active shoppers in their markets, and ask questions of their classified site partner if and when their active shopper tally trends downward.

Second, the classified sites have a responsibility to help dealers maximize the return on investment (ROI) they achieve from their classified site advertising packages. Both AutoTrader.com and Cars.com are doing a better job of being more consultative and collaborative with their dealer clients. They've recognized that many dealers have yet to achieve "advanced pixel proficiency" and the pathway to better online used vehicle merchandising performance and sales isn't always simply a matter of spending more money.

It's like what ecommerce director Kevin Frye at Wyler Automotive, Cincinnati, indicated in the last chapter: Dealers often have to turn inward and reinvent the people and processes that lead to "advanced pixel proficiency" before they are able to realize, and count on, an acceptable ROI from their classified site partners.

I should add there's good news here, too. Today's technology and tools have made the reinvention-oriented road to "advanced pixel proficiency" a less challenging puzzle for dealers. We now have the data and metrics to know which puzzle pieces matter the most and the tools to identify when one or more of these critical pieces goes missing.

Once again, though, it's incumbent that dealers recognize that you, and no one else, own the responsibility of putting this "advanced pixel pro-ficiency" puzzle together and keeping it there. "It isn't about writing a check," says Jared Hamilton, CEO of DrivingSales.com. "Your team has to be maximizing the opportunities."

I like how Jack Anderson, used vehicle director at West Herr Auto Group, Buffalo, N.Y., thinks about what it takes to build and maintain "advanced pixel proficiency" on classified sites and beyond:

"I call it 'the customer voting with his mouse,'" Anderson says. "Nothing happens until a customer votes with his mouse. You can think you've got a good car, and a good price and good pictures. But until someone clicks on it on the Internet, you've got nothing.

"We have three different worlds online," he contin-ues. "There are the classified sites, Cars.com and AutoTrader.com, and westherr.com. We live by the SRPs and VDPs on each one. I don't think there are many dealers that do that.

"In my world, if you're not managing the metrics on any of those three sites, it's a mistake. You're cutting one leg off the three-legged stool. Ultimately, you'd love your vehicle to perform on all three sites. But if you see it not performing on one site, you can still look and ask what you can do to change the outcome."

I liken a dealer's responsibility for "advanced pixel proficiency" to the role good parents should play with their children. The best parents check in with their children every morning. They want to get a read on each child—Do they seem okay? Is anything bothering them? Are they ready for the day ahead?

Good parents also recognize that each child is different. Among my three sons, two might be considered "morning people" while the third hits his stride later in the day. I also know each requires a different mix of conversation and questions if I sense something's clearly hanging heavy on their minds. I know how much I can press each one if, as a parent, I need to understand why one may seem "off" on a given day.

This is the kind of approach good dealers take to their used vehicles. They devote time every day to size up how well their cars are performing in the market. Like children, some used vehicles require more attention than others to make sure they're "right" on any given day.

MAXIMIZING YOUR "MOMENTS OF TRUTH"

In the Internet world, there's a lot of talk about the "moment of truth" for online vehicle shoppers. The phrase typically means that specific point in time when a buyer's mouse click signals purchase intent.

On classified sites like AutoTrader.com and Cars. com, this "moment of truth" occurs after online shoppers set parameters for a type of vehicle or a specific model and launch a search for those cars.

The first page they see, known as the search results page (SRP), typically offers between 25 and 50 different used vehicles, depending on the classified site. (**Note:** About 26 percent of online vehicle shoppers "price sort" their searches and SRP listings, according to AutoTrader.com. The majority, however, scroll up and down the SRP to scan vehicle listings. On average, online used vehicle shoppers only view two SRPs for each vehicle search query they submit (e.g., they go "two-deep").

A "moment of truth" on classified sites occurs when an online shopper viewing an SRP clicks on a listing for a specific car. This "click-through" means the shopper sees something they like about the vehicle, and they want to know more. The page that delivers this deeper-dive look into a specific car is called the vehicle details page (VDP).

A dealership's SRP to VDP conversion rate is what I refer to as the "money metric" in the online merchandising of used vehicles on classified sites (see box, this page, for AutoTrader.com and Cars.com benchmarks).

It's the online equivalent of an "up" in the show-room—someone who's expressed more than a passing interest in your vehicle and dealership.

SRP/VDP Dealer Benchmarks

The conversion rates from vehicle listings on search results pages (SRPs) to vehicle details pages (VDPs) vary between AutoTrader.com and Cars.com. The variance owes to the differences in form and format of each classified site.

Here are SRP-to-VDP conversion benchmarks velocity dealers use to ensure their online used vehicle merchandising maximizes the "moments of truth" for their cars:

AutoTrader.com: 1.5 – 2.5 percent

Cars.com: 2.5 - 3.5 percent

Note: These benchmarks serve as guides velocity dealers use to determine the level of shopper activity and interest in their vehicles. The specific conversion rates can vary by local market area, the classified site merchandising package a dealer chooses, as well as changes the classified sites make to their platforms to enhance the customer experience.

"We call it a virtual demo," Anderson says. "I've got someone test driving my car on their computer. I've got an up."

This is why Anderson and other velocity dealers pay close attention to the SRP to VDP conversion counts they get from the classified sites. They recognize that they won't get drill-down looks on specific cars (the VDP) unless their used vehicles show up on the SRPs online shoppers see as the "moment of truth" approaches. They understand that more VDPs typically translate to a greater number of showroom sales. They make it a point to maximize the "moments of truth" or VDPs their used vehicles generate.

"I look at my SRPs and VDPs every day," says Marc Ray vice president and partner at Grogan's Towne Chrysler, Toledo. "I look at them and get excited because that's what's going to put money in my pocket."

BUILDING YOUR VDP FACTORY

It's easy to spot a dealership where "advanced pixel proficiency" has become the new order of day for their online merchandising efforts.

The dealers themselves track SRP/VDP conversions. They reinvent the people and processes that contribute to increasing the number of times the "moment of truth" will occur on their cars.

In other words, they've turned their dealerships into VDP factories.

They've become students of the way the packaging and pricing of used vehicles online has a direct effect on their VDP counts and other online metrics. They've used this critical data to calibrate their online merchandising investments with their broader goals for used vehicle inventory turns, sales volumes and ROI.

I would suggest three foundational principles for dealers who seek to turn their dealerships into VDP factories—efficiency, elegance and effectiveness. Here's a more detailed look at each:

Efficiency: Velocity dealers today recognize a used vehicle isn't really for sale in today's Internet-driven marketplace unless a prospective shopper can see it online. Second, they understand that speed matters—time lost to taking pictures or writing descriptions hurts the ROI and profitability potential on a car.

For these reasons, many dealers have taken the following steps to maximize efficiencies as they craft the "right" online presentation for their used vehicles:

1. **Get photos up quickly.** Used car director Phil McDonald of Hudson Nissan, North Charleston, S.C., aims to list vehicles within 24 to 48 hours of acquiring them via auction or trade-in.

"We'll take two or three photos every morning of trade-ins we believe will clear," he says. "We'll run the cars through our car wash and take a couple basic pictures. We put a wrap on the listing that says, 'fresh inventory, more pictures to come.'"

For auction purchases, McDonald often uses photos from the auction provider or selling dealer to get a car posted online quickly.

The same is true at Mike Shaw Automotive dealerships, says COO Scott James of the Denver-based group. "I can't have a car that gets here Friday and not appear online until Tuesday," he says. "That's four or five days of no return.

"Ideally, I'd like to have my cars front-line ready and online with pictures in 48 hours," says James, who estimates about 50 percent of the vehicles fully meet the benchmark.

Jared Hamilton at DrivingSales.com puts it succinctly: "If the car doesn't have photos, it's not for sale."

2. **Use technology to help write vehicle descriptions.** It's important that dealers recognize the way classified sites display the comments and descriptions for used vehicle listings. On the SRP page, the description functions as a short-hand, character count-limited review of the car. On the VDP page, online shoppers see a more detailed description.

Today's technology and tools can help dealers efficiently create descriptions that fit the format classified sites require and maximize a vehicle's ROI and profitability potential.

At Don Ayres Honda, Fort Wayne, Ind., a used vehicle manager touches up vehicle descriptions generated by an automated description-writing tool to speedup this part of the online merchandising process, says Jim Bell, Internet performance and marketing manager.

"He puts his own spin in the first 150 characters— whether it's a one owner car or has new tires," Bell says.

The need for greater efficiencies in online merchandising of used vehicles is prompting some velocity dealers to hire digital content specialists and on-staff photographers to do these important jobs.

At Mike Shaw's Toyota store, "we've hired a photographer on staff to get the job done," Scott says. "You want to avoid situations where someone in detail takes pictures but no one follows up, or you have a third-party take pictures but they only come around once or twice a week."

Elegance: For the most part, classified sites are more about the car than the dealership. However, from the SRP to the VDP, and from one vehicle listing to another, dealers should be cognizant of what their listings convey about their dealerships and the brands they represent.

In many ways, the principles for effective merchandising of vehicles on a dealer's physical lot apply online. Simply, your stuff has to look good and read well to maximize your SRP/VDP conversion rates.

To address this, many dealers aim for consistency in descriptions and photos across all their vehicle listings on classified sites.

"We use the same angle on all of our cars on the first photo," says Bell at Don Ayres Honda. "It's off the left-front corner panel with our building in the background."

Dealer Lee Payne of Planet Honda, Denver, takes advantage of a lot of sunny days and a rooftop spot that offers a clean background and mountain skyline. "We've looked and compared those pictures to other dealers who use a photo booth," Payne says. "We like ours better. We think showing them outside in natural light shows off the car better."

Effectiveness: Even with advances in technology and online merchandising metrics, it's still largely impossible to know, with a great degree of certainty, why the "moment of truth" occurs on a given vehicle.

Unfortunately, neither AutoTrader.com nor Cars.com can climb inside the mind of an online shopper to know what's really firing the neurons that trip the "I want to see this car" trigger.

We don't know, for example, whether it simply is the "right" car at the "right" price for a particular buyer, or whether other factors, such as the way a dealer has packaged and positioned the vehicle listing, that spurred the click-through to see the car.

But we do know this: A vehicle listing's position on the SRP has a significant impact on its likelihood to generate a VDP. Similarly, the quality and number of photos and a vehicle's color are also prime VDP drivers (see box, next page, for AutoTrader.com data).

Because of these dynamics, velocity dealers who have built VDP factories say it's essential to minimize the unknowns—that is, they seek to do all aspects of online merchandising well, and then they "inspect what they expect."

"You want to make sure everything else is a given and the thing you'll dial to adjust traffic is your price," says Anderson at West Herr. "To make sure that price is your only adjustment mechanism, you have to make the assumption that everything else is good.

"You have to have good pictures, good descriptions and timely processes for getting cars on the web. You can't make your price the adjustment factor if there are too many other variables you haven't controlled," he says. "We've made a big effort to control the other factors so we can assume that we can look at SRPs and VDPs and know all we need

Factors That Drive VDP Counts

The following data highlights how a used vehicle's positioning and packaging affect the number of times online vehicle shoppers will click on a car's search results page (SRP) to view its vehicle details page (VDP) to learn more about the unit:

Positioning: Some classified sites are moving to rewarding dealers who offer more robust used vehicle merchandising (e.g., a full complement of photos, descriptions, video, etc.) with better placement for their vehicle listings. The idea: The better the merchandising, the higher the placement. Currently AutoTrader.com shows a marked SRP/VDP conversion lift for listings that consistently appear among the top 10 SRP listings.

Packaging: Listings with 27 photos average a 2.6 percent conversion rate; nine photos, 1.74 percent; three photos, 1.4 percent. Similarly, vehicle listings with a "reduced price" flag or a "newly listed" tag gain a 1.2 percent and .94 percent lift in conversion rates, respectively.

Color: Black vehicles enjoy a .96 percent lift in conversions, followed by charcoal (.69 percent), orange (.49 percent), blue (.21 percent) and gray (.18 percent) vehicles.

to adjust is price to get the conversions I'm looking for."

On a daily basis, Anderson and inventory control specialists or managers at each dealership will monitor SRP/VDP conversions for specific cars. Their inventory management system notes single-day and five-day SRP/VDP conversion trends for every car. Anderson's team targets an average 2.5 percent conversion rate to maximize each car's "moments of truth."

"That's the sweet spot," Anderson says. If a car isn't hitting the conversion range, managers drill deeper to double-check whether the vehicle's packaging, positioning or price is the problem.

"At that point, we know we need to make an adjustment," he says. "The first thing you need to do is make sure the car comes up in searches. If it doesn't, either the price is wrong and it's showing up on the third or fourth SRP page, or they're just not searching for the car in general.

"Then you check all the other stuff—the pictures, the description, the listed options. If everything's good, we'll look at price."

It's also possible that, at the end of this exercise, the problem may be the car itself. "Sometimes you could just have the wrong vehicle," Anderson says. "In my market, if you have a Cadillac STS and it doesn't have heated seats, you'll have trouble selling it."

If nothing else, it should be clear to dealers that "advanced pixel proficiency" isn't a cakewalk. Hence the sentiment noted above that all of this is "a hell of a lot of work."

It should also be clear that dealers who want to maximize the "moments of truth" their used vehicles generate and become VDP factories will likely need to reinvent the processes, if not the people, they rely on to ensure their online merchandising efforts harmonize with their goals for used vehicle ROI and profitability.

REINVENTION ROADBLOCK: ATTRIBUTION AND ITS DISCONTENTS

Joe Pistell has an ongoing debate with his dealer about spending money on classified sites like Auto-Trader.com and Cars.com.

Pistell believes the investments on these sites are absolutely essential for dealer Todd Caputo's three upstate New York dealerships to be successful. Caputo, on the other hand, isn't sold on the idea.

'In the marketing world, we're realizing it's mission critical to be advertising on the classified sites," says Pistell, marketing director for Sun Auto Group, Cicero, N.Y. "But Todd is convinced it's a complete waste of time to be on AutoTrader.com and Cars.

com. The problem is he can't see these customers. For him, it's 'show me the money.' I'll say, 'the customers are there,' but to him it's like they're invisible."

The debate at Sun mirrors discussions that frequently occur at dealerships across the country:

The Dealer: "The Internet is supposed to be an eminently track-able marketing medium. We should be seeing more leads from classified sites and a clearer-cut return on investment (ROI) from the checks we send them every month."

The Manager: "I know, boss. But I don't think we can afford to *not* be there. Given the way people shop online, these sites play a key role in helping customers find our cars and us."

At some dealerships, this discussion leads to a dealer-driven decision to eliminate classified sites from their online marketing and merchandising mix. The dealer concludes it's time to "go it alone." Often, this decision is followed by redeploying this investment in search engine marketing (SEM) and other online advertising efforts.

At other dealerships, the discussion leads to détente, just as it does at Sun Auto Group. Caputo and Pistell agree to disagree—and they work harder to "turn the light on in a dark room and learn how these people find us and how we can master the digital marketplace," Pistell says.

In this chapter, I'd like to shed some light into this dark room.

To me, the debate over the ROI from classified sites highlights a fundamental misunderstanding of how today's online shoppers look for used cars. In addition, I also believe the decision to "go it alone" often unnecessarily turns dealers into competitors with classified sites for the online attention and time of used vehicle shoppers. This automatically makes the redeployment of investments to SEM and other online advertising a steeper hill—and one I don't believe the vast majority of dealers should climb in all cases, particularly when the chief purpose is to maximize the ROI and profitability in used vehicles.

I've come to these conclusions after dozens of discussions with dealers and careful examination of the ways today's Internet-enabled buyers search and shop for used vehicles. The following are the four factors I believe dealers should consider *before* they opt out of classified sites and decide to "go it alone."

1. **The Attribution Disconnect:** Like any business owner, dealers believe if they spend X they should get Y in return. In the pre-Internet days, this desire to attribute sales to specific marketing expenditures had dealers like me tallying up the showroom traffic and sales every Saturday to determine whether our weekly newspaper ad performed well.

The Internet takes attribution to a new level. Dealers have come to expect that any investment in online marketing and merchandising should generate a certain amount of conversions, click-throughs, website traffic and active leads.

The problem with classified sites is the full scope of attention and influence they achieve with online used vehicle shoppers isn't as fully attributable as dealers expect. As we noted in Chapter 17, the majority of shoppers who view specific vehicles on classified sites don't "raise their hand" in a way that would lend itself to a clear-cut ROI analysis.

On AutoTrader.com, only a small number of shoppers (3 percent) will e-mail a dealership after viewing a vehicle listing, and an even smaller segment (1 percent) will click to visit a dealer's website. Most are far more likely to view a vehicle listing and simply show up at the dealership—with many of those shoppers using Google to scope a dealer's website and inventory *after* they've landed on a car they like on classified sites.

As dealers calculate the ROI from classified sites, they will only count these "direct" leads and give little, if any, credit to other indirect benefits that their classified sites provide.

This dynamic leads to the tug-of-war between dealers and marketing teams over the ROI and efficacy of investments on classified sites. It's also the reason guys like Pistell at Sun Motor Group continue to push back when their dealers suggest they pull the plug on their classified site investments.

"The days of AutoTrader.com and Cars.com serving as a lead generation for dealers are long gone," says Bryan Armstrong, e-commerce director for Volkswagen of South Town, Sandy Point, Utah. "They are really research sites. The only reason people are going there is to find out whether or not your car is priced competitive to other cars. I absolutely believe you need to have a presence on these sites."

2. **The FireFly Effect.** The latest industry surveys suggest that today's online vehicle shoppers (a blend of new and used car intenders) visit nearly 20 different websites as they decide the vehicle they want to buy and the dealership from which they wish to make a potential purchase. These online visits typically include stops to roughly two different dealership websites. The classified sites also rank highly (and repeatedly) among the go-to online vehicle shopper destinations.

"Dealers often think there's a single online path to a sale for a customer," Pistell says. "They think the customer starts at Point A and follows a direct line to the dealership.

"It's much more like a firefly," he says. "They're here, and then they're invisible. They light up and they're over there. Then they're invisible. They light up, and they're 20 yards away. The reality is they bounce all over the place."

This "firefly effect" owes to the shopper's need to narrow the list of used vehicle choices and dealers to a manageable list, and the need to compare vehicles and prices during this process.

The need to compare cars is the chief reason, I believe, that the classified sites like AutoTrader.com and Cars.com remain highly useful and relevant for online used vehicle shoppers. They offer the most depth and width of used vehicle inventory available, from both dealers and private sellers.

Dealers who opt to "go it alone," and redeploy their investments in SEM and other online advertising, will likely fall short of satisfying this "need to compare" as they attract and direct customers to their own websites.

"When the shopper goes to AutoTrader.com and Cars.com, he instinctively knows he's got one dealer competing against the other," Pistell says. "If he's on a car dealer's website, he can't shop other dealers."

A related "go it alone" problem: Dealers who ditch classified sites effectively eliminate platforms that provide additional visibility for their vehicles and lead these "firefly-like" customers to their showroom doors.

"If you choose not to be visible on AutoTrader.com or Cars.com, you lose the opportunity to create a path to your store," Pistell says. "Dealers need to remember there isn't one path, there are multiple paths for today's shoppers. Every time you reduce your visibility, whether it's traditional or digital media, you cut off a path to your store."

3. **SEM Pitfalls:** A dealer's decision to eliminate classified sites and "go it alone" often triggers a shift to search engine marketing (SEM) to attract online used vehicle shoppers to the dealer's website and inventory. This form of online marketing typically requires dealers to identify the most commonly used keywords[8] used when customers search for used vehicles, and position dealer website pages and pay-per-click (PPC) advertising for maximum engagement.

There are two significant hurdles dealers who "go it alone" must overcome as they play the SEM game:

The Competition: Generally, the volume of "short-tail" searches for used vehicles far outstrips the volume of "long-tail" searches. This stands to reason as "short-tail" queries often occur at the

---

[8] Keywords typically fall into two buckets:

"Short-tail" terms: These keywords are more generic and broad, and typically reflect the interests of online shoppers who are in the early stages of their hunt for a used vehicle. Sample terms would include "used vehicles Chicago" or "used SUVs Chicago."

"Long-tail" terms: These keywords offer more specificity and typically reflect the interests of online shoppers who are further along in the research and purchase process and have a better idea of the specific type of used vehicle they want. Sample terms would include "used 2008 Chevy Tahoe Chicago" or "certified pre-owned Chevy Tahoe Chicago."

start of an online shopper's used vehicle research and purchase process.

Dealers who "go it alone" and opt to play the "short-tail" game effectively chose to compete directly with classified sites and other lead generation companies who typically saturate this segment of the market. This means the costs to gain visibility via PPC ads is high. Likewise, the time and effort to achieve visibility in organic listings is significant, given larger, more established players have effectively "owned" this positioning for a longer period of time.

There are signs that "long tail" searches are gaining in volume, and may represent an emerging opportunity for SEM-focused dealers. However, these "long-tail" searches are still far fewer in number than their "short-tail" counterparts. Similarly, success in the "long-tail" game requires careful calibration and optimization of dealership website inventory listings and landing pages to attract and keep customers—and even that might not be enough to satisfy these shoppers (see next factor, below).

The Experience: Whether SEM-minded dealers focus on "short-tail" or "long-tail" search terms, the end game almost always should be to bring a used vehicle shopper to the dealership website and a specific, keyword-optimized landing page that features the car(s) the shopper wants to see.

The problem here, as noted earlier, is that most dealership websites and inventories don't currently satisfy the typical online used vehicle shopper's desire to quickly scan and compare a bunch of used vehicles in a single shot.

Pistell offers the following to illustrate the point:

"Let's say you have two Nissan Sentras on your lot. One is a 2011, the other a 2006. The shopper goes to Google and types in 'used Nissan Sentra for sale (city).' The shopper clicks on the dealer's pay-per-click ad, goes to the dealership website and sees two Nissan Sentras. That's it. Two cars. There's no opportunity to look at differences in colors, features, options or mileage, much less other cars. The shopper clicks the back button and Ka-ching!, the money goes down the toilet. There isn't any opportunity to show the shopper that you have Altimas, Chevrolets and other cars.

"The depth of the inventory is like a flame to a moth. The shopper is attracted to inventory and if you don't have bulk, size or scale, or the tools on your website to facilitate the experience, then stand-alone search marketing is extremely inefficient."

I tested the premise that the SEM "experience" for shoppers is less than satisfying with a "long-tail" Google search for "used 2009 Chevy Tahoe Chicago." Here's what I found:

- Two of the three top-of-page PPC listings came from General Motors (via the *www.GMCerti-*

fied.com, and ***www.chevydealers.com*** sites). The third came from ***www.chevydriveschicago. com,*** a co-op site for Chicago and Northwest Indiana-area dealers. Of these three PPC listings, only the ***www.chevydriveschicago.com*** ad mentioned "Tahoe" in the text. I clicked the ad and landed on a page for 2012 Chevy Tahoes, with no reference to the 2009 model I wanted to see. I hit the "back" button on my browser.

- Seven of the eight PPC listings on the right side of the search results page came from dealers (the No. 3 listing came from Cars.com).

- I clicked the first PPC ad for a dealer in Lisle, a Chicago suburb. I was encouraged by the "Used Chevy Tahoe" and "view our certified pre-owned Chevy Tahoe inventory" headline and ad text. My click-through took me to a landing page with an error message, "We're unable to locate a vehicle."

- I skipped the second ad because its text said nothing about used vehicles or Tahoes.

- I clicked the third ad, for Cars.com, because it promised more than 12,000 used Tahoes and the ability to "contact local Chicago sellers today!" I landed on a page with 912 available used Chevy Tahoes.

- I clicked the fourth ad, from CarMax, due to its pledge of "used Chevy Tahoes at low, no-haggle prices." The landing page showed me a listing of 150 Tahoes.

- The fifth ad came from a Barrington, Ill., dealer and offered a "used Chevrolet Tahoe in stock." I landed on a page that listed a 1999 Chevrolet Tahoe and a 2011 Chevrolet Tahoe. The page also offered me a prominent "value your trade" tool.

- The remaining three ads came from other Chicago-area dealers and two specifically mentioned "Tahoe" in the ad text. My click-throughs took me to landing pages where I saw one 2009 Chevy Tahoe at one dealership, and a 2007 Chevy Tahoe at the other.

To me, this test offered three key take-aways:

First, it's apparent that some dealers *do* understand the SEM game, and they're doing their best to offer up vehicles that match my interest as a shopper. Some were better at this than others, of course. But I was encouraged by signs of "advanced pixel proficiency" in the PPC ads, even if they didn't all satisfy my need to see at least one used 2009 Chevy Tahoe.

Second, the test effectively demonstrates Pistell's point that inventory size matters when it comes to SEM. As a shopper, there's no doubt I would have spent more time on the Cars.com and CarMax sites because they offered me a lot more cars to evaluate and compare.

Third, the test underscores the many moving parts dealers who "go it alone" must master as they rely on SEM and PPC ads to drive shoppers to their used vehicle inventories.

A recommendation: Dealers should regularly review the effectiveness of their SEM efforts, particularly if they pay a third-party agency to handle this work.

I should add that I also scanned the top 10 organic search listings. Of those, five search results came from sites that offered classified listings. They were (in order) Cargurus.com (#1 position), Yahoo! (#5), KBB.com (#6), EveryCarListed.com (#8), and Auto-Trader.com (#10). Three of the remaining organic listings (listings #2-#4) highlighted YouTube videos from dealers, all of which were posted between 2009 and 2011, and highlighted vehicles that were no longer available. Two listings came from local dealers (#7 and #9 positions) and offered links to optimized website pages for Chevy Tahoes. One dealer's landing page took me to a history of the Chevy Tahoe; the other dealer's page offered a used 2009 Chevy Tahoe but lacked any photos.

4. **Classified Site Customer Service:** I am keenly aware that dealer frustration with classified sites goes beyond the cost to advertise used vehicle inventory on these platforms and the difficulties attributing and calculating the ROI they deliver.

I will say, however, that I'm convinced and confident that executives at AutoTrader.com and

Cars.com understand they need to do a better job enhancing the value proposition they offer dealers.

At AutoTrader.com, for example, the company has spent significant resources to ensure their sales and product teams help dealers do a better job of using their partnership to achieve "advanced pixel proficiency" and sell more used vehicles.

I would boil these efforts into what I would call the "3C's of the AutoTrader.com value proposition:"

Competency: The company has shifted its field teams to serve as consultants rather than just representatives who sell advertising packages to dealers. They have helped dealers understand the value of the vehicle details page (VDP) conversion as the "money metric." They now provide detailed Scorecards that highlight merchandising successes and inefficiencies for dealers.

AutoTrader.com is also sending its field teams to NADA University to gain a deeper understanding of the car business and to enhance their credibility and competency as consultants to dealer partners.

Caring: In the past two years, AutoTrader.com has spent more time focusing on hiring field representatives who are motivated by helping their dealer clients, not just selling more services. This initiative flows directly from a top-level understanding that dealer loyalty isn't a given. It's a right that's earned by going the extra mile and lending a helping hand when needed.

Commitment: AutoTrader.com has adopted pay plans that reward its field team based on the improved performance of their dealer partners, not just their sales totals. This is welcome news for dealers, all of whom understand the age-old truth that "pay plans determine behavior."

Cars.com also understands its success depends on its ability to continually add value to its relationships with dealers, and help them along their respective roads to reinvention.

"Our goal is to be a trusted consultant to our dealers in growing their businesses with online car shoppers – today, that's nearly everyone," says Mitch Golub, Cars.com founder and president. He notes the mission includes training programs that help dealers harmonize in-store processes to meet the needs of online buyers, manage their online reputations more effectively, maximize their Cars.com investments and reach customers in the social media and mobile spaces.

"We've made a lot of investments in data-mining and analytics to help dealers make sure they're targeting the right audiences and making their marketing investments more efficient and effective," Golub says.

I don't want this chapter to discourage dealers who firmly believe that a "go it alone" strategy is the best next step for their dealerships. Rather, the intention is to highlight why I believe this approach proves more problematic than profitable for most dealers.

I also recognize some dealers will dismiss this chapter as mere cheerleading on behalf of classified sites, the biggest of which just happens to be my current employer, AutoTrader.com. I respect this position and hope there's at least a nugget or two here that will make their "go it alone" strategy more successful.

REINVENTION ROADBLOCK: THE RISING TIDE OF TRANSPARENCY

Dealers have long been aware that price matters to car buyers.

In virtually every market, there's been at least one dealer who touts his dealership as the "home of the low price" or "the low price leader" or "the place that beats any advertised price."

In many cases, these marketing pitches were just that—a pitch to draw in potential buyers. These stores didn't consistently offer low prices and, if one were to examine the deal jackets, I'd suspect the transaction prices weren't always the lowest in the market. I'd also wager the deals with the lowest transaction prices had more to do with the negotiation skills of a customer than the dealer's pricing strategy.

As many dealers now understand, the Internet has changed some of these pricing dynamics. There are more dealers who are pricing their vehicles "in the market" and "on the money" because the Internet provides easy and efficient access to vehicle pricing information. It has spurred consumer expectations for pricing transparency from car dealers.

"If you don't price the car correctly, it won't sell," says John Worthington, Internet sales manager and general manager for Doug Henry Automotive, Tarboro, N.C. "Your pricing has to be transparent."

This rising tide of consumer expectations for pricing transparency hit a high point in late 2011. That's when TrueCar, a company that promised vehicle shoppers the "best local price" and a "better car buying experience," took its platform for pricing transparency to a national scale.

Buoyed by a reported $200 million in equity financing, the company announced its mission to change the way consumers buy cars.

The company invited consumers to its website where, in just a few clicks, a would-be car buyer could see a spread of market-based prices for vehicles on a bell curve. Consumers could see if a vehicle's price was "great," "good" or "above market." They could then click a "locate dealer" icon and find a store that would sell the vehicle for the price presented on the website. (Participating dealers paid TrueCar a fee ($299 for new cars, $399 for used cars) when they closed deals with these customers.)

TrueCar touted its purchase process as a new source of "radical clarity" for vehicle buyers. The company's CEO, Scott Painter, said TrueCar's process would effectively eliminate the need for salespeople in dealer showrooms.

"The car sells itself at that point. It's effectively a commodity," Painter told *Automotive News* in August, 2011.

To dealers, of course, these were the equivalent of fighting words. They didn't like the idea that an outside company might price their cars and their customers for them. Further, they didn't like the idea that TrueCar's model stripped them of their ability to negotiate with customers.

In addition, dealers didn't like the effect TrueCar's presence had in their market on customers and vehicle prices.

Here's one perspective from a Chicago-area Chevrolet dealer: "TrueCar had a devastating effect on the market almost immediately. It was the race to the bottom for the dealer who was the biggest liar. When the customer goes there, one of two things would happen. They baffle the customer with all kinds of baloney and raise the price, or they piss off the customer and the customer leaves. Then, the customer migrates to a different product. The sad part is, the customer evolves into a better buyer for the next person he talks to."

These were the dynamics that led to the big "True-Car Controversy" in 2011. Dealers rallied and launched a surprisingly unified and effective effort to stop TrueCar's advance into the marketplace.

In online auto industry forums, dealers openly expressed their disdain and dissatisfaction for TrueCar and its call for greater transparency in dealership pricing and processes. They urged the reportedly more than 5,700 dealers who had signed on as TrueCar partners to dump the company. They called TrueCar "evil" and CEO Scott Painter, the "devil."

Dealers also alleged the company had improperly accessed their customer data to retrieve and reveal actual transaction prices for specific cars in specific markets. Dealers viewed this as a possible violation of consumer privacy laws and a sure-fire way to diminish dealer profits.

The dust-up cost TrueCar about 2,000 participating dealers, according to industry press reports. Further, dealer-driven push-back triggered notable changes in TrueCar's business model:

- It no longer touts "actual transaction prices" for vehicles. Instead, it suggests a "target price" for car buyers, much like data offered on sites like Edmunds.com and Kbb.com.

- In many states, it no longer offers a pay-for-performance compensation plan for dealers. The company has switched to more of a subscription-for-leads payment model, much like other lead provider groups.

- The company has hired long-time industry players to smooth out relationships with dealers and promote the company's broker-like services as a win-win for dealers and car buyers. "They're definitely coming back with their hats in hand," says a Virginia dealer who dropped out of the TrueCar program while the controversy raged.

If I were keeping score, I would say it's Dealers: 1, TrueCar: 0.

But I don't believe dealers have seen the end of TrueCar, nor have they seen the last of companies who aim to provide vehicle shoppers exactly what they want—a fair price on a car and a buying process that preys less on their emotions and more on their preferences.

A prediction: In the next three to five years, there will be a company that successfully makes the promise of pricing transparency and a better car buying experience a reality for vehicle shoppers and dealers on a national scale.

I recognize this prediction may anger some dealers. But, if we're honest with ourselves, I think we can all agree that this marketplace shift is inevitable.

Consider the efficiencies the Internet has already created for vehicle buyers: They no longer need to spend a Saturday at multiple dealerships looking at and, possibly, test driving cars. They can shop cars online at home or work, via a computer or smartphone.

Industry stats say online vehicle shoppers visit nearly 20 different websites as they decide on the type of car they might want to purchase and the price they can afford to pay. A company like TrueCar would make this process even more efficient by offering credible vehicle prices, related research resources (e.g., dealer and vehicle ratings) and dealers who are willing to honor the pledge of providing more transparent prices and a no-hassle buying experience.

To me, this is the broader message that got lost in the "TrueCar Controversy." While dealers were fuming about TrueCar and its CEO, they didn't often step back and consider the larger implications the company presents for increased pricing transparency for automotive retailing in the years ahead.

"TrueCar opens everybody's eyes to the idea and benefit of a transparent price and process," says dealer Andrew DiFeo of Hyundai of St. Augustine, Fla. "If it's not TrueCar, it's going to be someone else."

I agree, and the implications from the "TrueCar Controversy" couldn't be more clear: The way forward for dealers requires embracing pricing transparency and offering a "better car buying experience" to remain relevant for car buyers today and tomorrow.

"Consumers want to play the game with the cards face up," says Mark Rikess, head of The Rikess Group, which advocates transparency-based pricing and sales processes for dealers. He points to demographic studies that suggest 60-plus percent of today's buyers are either women or part of Generation Y.

"These buyers dislike negotiation and they'll even pay a little bit more to not negotiate," Rikess says.

Interestingly, dealers who participated in TrueCar's network affirm Rikess' point. They note that while a competitive price is important, their sales processes made the difference in ensuring an acceptable profit margin in TrueCar-generated deals.

"We used TrueCar at a high level and sold 10 customers every month," says Tom Drummond, Internet sales manager at Ferguson Buick-GMC, Norman, Okla., which sells 200-plus new/used vehicles each month.

Did you make any money on those deals? "Oh, yeah," Drummond says. "We made an average of $1,200 in front-end gross a copy and another $1,600 in F&I profit."

How'd you make it work? "We didn't fight with the customer over the TrueCar process," he adds. "We went in and aggressively priced our vehicles to offer the top-of-mind best value. We weren't often the cheapest out there but we always made sure we had the best value—the best equipment at the best price. We didn't use cheater cars."

"We saw an opportunity to be counter-intuitive compared to other dealers," echoes Joshua Friedman, Internet sales manager at Heritage Chevrolet, Richmond, Va. "For us, the race wasn't to the bottom. It was a race to integrity. We found TrueCar deals offered a decent return on investment."

"Price isn't the only factor," says Chad Lemieux, corporate used car director for the Los Angeles-based, The Car Group. "Do you shop at Wal-Mart or Target? You pay more at Target but it's a much better buying experience. Dealers don't have to be a Nordstrom, you can be something in between."

I understand why many dealers resist this evolutionary shift in the car business toward greater pricing transparency. It runs against the grain of everything traditional dealers were taught about how to price and sell cars. It can be painful to accept that companies like TrueCar might be a necessary adjunct to price cars and customers—two aspects of the business dealers have long controlled.

"We're paying for the sins of our past," says DiFeo, a 37-year-old dealer who grew up in the business.

"Before the Internet, we had all the information and a good majority of dealers abused that."

In DiFeo's view, the "pricing games" of the past have seeded sufficient distrust in dealers that buyers now seek out what they perceive as credible sources to determine a fair price to pay for a car, whether it's TrueCar, Edmunds, KBB.com or other vehicle price validators. In this way, the "market of efficient information" is setting price expectations, not dealers themselves.

"Maybe through hundreds of thousands of dollars of advertising and branding a dealer or dealer group might be able to say, 'we're good people and we have a good price,'" DiFeo says. "Maybe that would prevent consumers from saying, 'I don't trust these people and I need to go to some third-party to validate the pricing.' I don't know if that could happen, but I do know that it's never going to go back to the way it was."

Next chapter: A close look at how dealers are working to establish a greater degree of trust and satisfaction with customers with more transparent sales processes.

REINVENTION IN ACTION:
DOCUMENTATION AS THE
NEW NEGOTIATION

Salesperson: *"Thank you for coming in today, Mr. Smith. We've got the 2010 Nissan Altima you wanted to see outside and ready for a test drive. Before we head out, I'd like to share a little information about our prices. We don't mark up our cars like other dealers, and offer big discounts. We price our cars to be competitive, which I'm sure you noticed in your research online.*

"After we test drive the car, I'll share a market survey report that shows how we priced the car. We'll also review the CARFAX report and the work we did in our service department to get the Altima

in tip-top shape for you. I'm confident you'll agree this car is a great value and a great ride. Here are the keys, let's go take this baby for spin."

This type of dialogue with customers is becoming more common as dealers across the country reinvent their sales processes to deliver a greater degree of transparency and maximize their return on investment (ROI) and profitability in used vehicles. It's an effective set-up for the following exchange that often occurs after a test drive:

Customer: *"I love this car. What can you do for me on the price?"*

Salesperson: *"Well, let's take a look at the market survey I promised before the test drive. As you can see, the RealDeal market survey shows your 2010 Altima is priced $1,200 below the two other Nissan Altimas available in the market, and this car has fewer miles than either of those.*

Now, I'm not telling you anything you don't already know. You did your homework and know that our Altima offers a great price and value.

Customer: *"You're right. But I'd still like to do better on the price."*

Salesperson: *"I understand. I mentioned earlier that we don't price our cars to negotiate discounts like other dealers. We price them exactly where they should be to meet the market and offer a great deal for you. Basically, we've taken the hassle of* *negotiating out of the equation. It's easier for you, and it's easier for us. The bottom line is, you can see from the market survey our price is better than fair, and I can't give you a discount."*

Customer: *"Well, okay. But you know what they say, 'it never hurts to ask.'"*

Salesperson: *"I hear you, Mr. Smith. I know it's probably a little weird to find a dealership that actually means it when they say they want to give you a great deal and an easy, no-hassle buying experience. But that's what makes us different from other dealers and, quite frankly, it's the reason I'm working here. Now, let's knock out the paperwork and get you home in your new car."*

I call this transparency-oriented reinvention of used vehicle sales processes "documentation as the new negotiation" for selling used cars. Velocity dealers say the "document, don't discount" mantra is a clear-cut winner that helps them address two new realities today's more efficient, Internet-driven marketplace has created:

1. **It's affirming for customers.** Beyond meeting customer expectations for transparency, which we outlined in the last chapter, the "documentation as the new negotiation" approach has a positive psychological effect for buyers. In the example above, Mr. Smith landed on the 2010 Nissan Altima because his own research showed it was the best deal for him in the market. The

salesperson's process and talk-track actively acknowledges and rewards Mr. Smith for his due diligence—and positions it as a principal reason the dealership cannot extend a discount.

"If we have a good price and there's a good presentation, the chances are small we'd discount the car anyway," says dealer Keith Kocourek of Kocourek Chevrolet, Wausau, Wis. He notes some customers will still ask, and maybe press, to get a discount. But they typically back off once they see the market survey and recognize Kocourek studies the market just like they do.

"They'll lay over and that's the end of it," he says.

Marc Ray, vice president and partner at Grogan's Towne Chrysler, Toledo, says his stores may make an occasional $100-$200 discount from their advertised prices—but it's a rare occurrence.

"When customers come in, it's about giving them proof of why my price is good and why they should pay what I'm asking," Ray says. "If we discount, it's only to give the customer a sense that they won. If you tell customers, 'this is it,' they understand."

2. **It protects dealer profit margins.** As we've noted in earlier chapters, many dealers recognize today's more efficient, Internet-driven marketplace requires competitive pricing on used vehicles to attract customers. They also

understand this price-efficient environment puts a greater degree of pressure on their front-end gross profit margins.

But many of these dealers miss how traditional, negotiation-based sales practices actually hurt their ROI and profit margin potential.

In January 2012, dealer Adam Claiborne at Fernandez Honda, San Antonio, wanted to figure out why, in spite of strong sales volumes, the store's front-end gross profit was suffering.

"I ran some numbers and found we were discounting close to $500 on every car," Claiborne says. "That just doesn't work. We were eroding our own gross when there's already a lot of pressure on it in the marketplace."

His solution: Adoption of the "documentation as the new negotiation" sales process. "I had a meeting with my used car manager and general sales manager. We started making sure that when we're doing our first pencil, we're presenting the evidence for our Internet Value Price.

"We went from discounting 70 percent of our cars to 50 percent in 10 days," Claiborne says.

In a month's time, the store saw a $45,000 lift in its gross profit on 90 deals—essentially a "put back" of the $500 per car the store had been losing through price discounts. "That's real money," Claiborne says.

The store hasn't eliminated every discount, but price reductions are far less frequent and, when they do occur, there's generally a good reason.

"You can't convince some customers and sometimes it just makes sense to do the deal that day—maybe we're getting a good trade or we have a finance opportunity," he says.

Claiborne and other velocity dealers note that they've changed their pay plans to reflect the reinvention toward "documentation as the new negotiation" for their sales teams.

These new pay plans make a fundamental shift: They reward sales teams for minimizing price discounts and maximizing their individual monthly sales totals.

For example, Claiborne pays sales people a base salary ($1,500/month average) and unit bonuses after they've sold eight vehicles. The bonuses increase with an individual's monthly sales volumes. In addition, he's created the "$250 Club" to keep sales teams focused on minimal discounts with customers (see box, next page).

"It's created a lot of stability in our sales team," Claiborne says. "Our guys get a little salary and once they hit eight units they get their bonuses. They come in each month knowing they'll make this much money, no matter how bad the business might be in a given month. That's unique in the car business where salespeople come in at

A Look Inside the "250 Club"

Dealer Adam Claiborne at Fernandez Honda, San Antonio, created the "$250 Club" to reward his sales team for minimizing price discounts with used vehicle customers.

The idea for the "$250 Club" came out of Claiborne's effort to increase the front-end margins on used vehicle sales. Here's how it works:

- Salespeople earn points on every deal, based on the difference between a vehicle's asking and transaction price. If there's no discount, a salesperson earns 250 points; if the discount is less than $250, the salesperson earns 125 points.

- At the end of the month, the four salespeople with the highest point totals earn $250 each, plus a dinner, tickets to the San Antonio Spurs playoff games, or a different "creative prize."

Claiborne credits the program for helping increase the store's monthly used vehicle front-end gross profits by $45,000. In addition, salespeople like the program because it's a fairer way to compensate them than traditional gross-based pay plans.

"The only thing salespeople really control is the discount," he says. "They don't control how much I pay to acquire and recondition the car. We actually control the gross.

"A guy may get 250 points when I only make $500. Another guy won't get any points if he discounts a car $500 and I make $3,500 because I was in the car right. He didn't set me up for that. Their goal is the presentation and presenting the evidence."

zero every month and you don't make a pay-check until you've sold seven cars."

Kocourek takes a similar, volume-focused approach to sales team compensation.

At his stores, sales teams must meet customer satisfaction index (CSI) scores to maximize their unit volume bonuses. Salespeople earn flats for up to nine vehicles, with retroactive bonuses that reach $350 per car at 30 sold units a month. If salespeople miss the 90 percent monthly CSI target, the per-car bonus amounts are 12 percent and 14 percent less.

"We've taken the mystery out of the pay plans," Kocourek says. "It's a modern-day Ponzi scheme where nobody loses."

3. **It creates a stronger, more stable sales team.**
   Velocity dealers say the adoption of "documentation as the new negotiation" is helping them change the culture and composition of their sales teams. They no longer need the hard-to-find blend of the tough negotiator with the gentle touch.

   Instead, they're able to tap into a pool of talent many traditional dealers wouldn't consider for their sales teams.

"It attracts salespeople that you'd never be able to attract before," Kocourek says. "As much as you and I don't like negotiating, salespeople don't like it either. I can hire a kid out of a pizza place and put them through our training process and have them out there selling cars and doing really well.

"They don't have to go through all the brain damage of negotiating back and forth and trying to trick people into paying too much," Kocourek says.

"Our society doesn't breed enough of the traditional negotiators any more to populate showroom floors. That's a huge pinch," says Mark Rikess, head of The Rikess Group, a Los Angeles-based firm that helps dealers with transparency-based sales processes.

"When you eliminate the negotiation piece, you open up your window for recruitment much wider," he says. "There are a lot of people with good natural sales skills that don't want to play the game of back and forth between the guest and desk." (See box, next page, for Rikess' tips to recruit transparency-minded sales talent.)

Claiborne at Fernandez Honda says his adoption of "documentation as the new negotiation" for selling used cars has "created a lot of stability" and less sales team turnover.

4. **It matches a dealer's interest in doing business in a different way.** "The fact of the matter is, this is the way I want to do business," Kocourek says. "It's the way I want to sell cars and buy cars.

Recruiting Transparency-Focused Sellers

Mark Rikess of The Rikess Group in Los Angeles offers the following pointers to help dealers recruit "transparency-minded" salespeople.

1. **Use Craigslist.** Rikess says this is a "go-to" medium for dealers to find individuals with good customer and natural sales skills who will thrive in a transparency-focused sales system. "Dealers should advertise for a "customer service representative" and note a preference for college-level education. The reason: The positioning attracts people with relevant retail experience.

2. **Ask your owners.** A quarterly e-mail to a store's past customers can convey a "if you like buying here, you'll love working here" message.

3. **Post available positions in your dealership.** This can be done via placards, posters, mirror hangars or kiosk videos that highlight opportunities and the pay/benefits packages the dealership offers.

Rikess also notes that "the best dealerships never recruit out of need. They recruit all the time."

That's the way I want to buy everything else I get. I'm just bringing that into my stores."

Marc Ray, vice president and partner at Grogan's Towne Chrysler, Toledo, believes "documentation as the new negotiation" gives him an edge with today's transparency-minded customers.

"They say consumers used to go to 3.5 dealerships, now it's 1.5," he says. "They're looking online for the cars they want. They're ending up at one store to look at them. The guy who is the most transparent, treats them the best and has the best process is going to get the business."

REINVENTION IN ACTION: THE "NEW RELIGION" FOR USED VEHICLE DEPARTMENTS

In early 2011, dealer W.C. Smith and general manager Bryan Hardman decided the time had come to embark on the road to reinvention at Monument Chevrolet in Pasadena, Texas.

The decision followed a sense that while they were doing okay in used vehicles, the store's performance could be better.

It wasn't an easy decision, particularly since they were considered top dogs in used vehicles by their peers. At 20 Group meetings, Monument's front-end gross profit average earned praise, respect and invitations to share their insights with other dealers.

"We were glad to be on the top of the page at our 20 Group and be invited to come talk to people," Smith says. "But we really wondered if we were missing something."

"From the outside, our sales and gross profits were good," Hardman says. "Inside, we were stewing. We saw the sales at Texas Direct. We started asking ourselves if there were other ways to do this."

The curiosity led to demos of inventory management tools and research into different retailing models to help take their monthly sales to the next level. So began their journey to velocity management and the road to reinvention.

"We decided to stock up on cars and price them to market," Smith says. "That's exactly what we did."

Within two months, however, both Smith and Hardman wondered if they'd made a seriously bad business decision.

"Our volume hadn't changed. Our grosses dropped and our inventory had ballooned," Smith says. "At the time, we thought we'd lost our minds 60 days prior. We said, 'this isn't working.' We basically lost our nerve."

The experience at Monument matches those of other dealers who adopt velocity principles and then find themselves spinning out on the road to reinvention. The reasons for the spin-outs often vary but they all share a common lineage: The dealers had not gone "all in" in their efforts to reinvent their used vehicle departments.

In fact, Hardman and Smith came to this understanding while asking themselves the "what went wrong?" questions after they'd hit the wall. Neither of these guys like failure and they still hadn't satisfied the gut-tugs that told them they were missing opportunities in their used vehicle business.

Rather than lick their wounds, Smith and Hardman doubled down. In January 2012, they started down the road to reinvention again. This time, though, they had a better understanding of the scale and scope of the effort.

"You can't just go buy some cars and price them to market and think that velocity just happens," Smith says. "There are some things in the velocity model that are diametrically opposed and intrinsically exclusive to the traditional dealership business model. It's a very holistic approach. The success doesn't come by adopting one or two principles and getting good at them.

"The key is to understand that this is a religious change. That's what separates the men from the boys. We're going from Christianity to Buddhism," Smith says. "It's a big deal. It affects everything you do and how you do it."

This "new religion" at Monument has yielded impressive results:

- The store's monthly used vehicle sales have increased 30 percent;

- The inventory turn has improved by 50 percent, from eight times to 12 times a year;

- Wholesale losses have disappeared, with only an occasional vehicle hitting 60 days of age;

- Front-end grosses run on par with those of top-performing velocity dealers;

- F&I income per sale has increased nearly 30 percent (thanks to market-based pricing that leaves financing room for warranties and other products);

- Profits in fixed operations have increased 20 percent due to additional reconditioning work.

Perhaps the most impressive aspect of Smith and Hardman's efforts is the time it took for them to achieve these results—just six months, roughly half the time it takes many dealers to embark on the road to reinvention and claim success. Even better, they achieved these performance improvements with largely the same people who have long worked at the dealership.

"We might have lost a six- or seven-car salesperson," Hardman says. "But we have the same people and managers as before, even with a big culture change."

I asked how they managed to make this change without the personnel shake-up that often occurs at other dealerships.

"We're a very regimented store," Smith says. "There are people that are not interested in working with us because of that. But we had the understanding this is a change in religion and one that does not look good when you get started. You've got to build into it."

"How were you able to get all this done in six months?," I asked.

"It takes commitment at two levels," Smith says. "The dealer or whoever is fronting the money for this experiment, and the used car manager who is out there making every single tactical decision about every piece of inventory.

"If you don't have the right people, it won't work. It takes the right people at all the right levels. Anybody that loses the faith will make this transition longer at a minimum. At a maximum, it can stall or make the transition fail.

'It's like the guys who sailed with Christopher Columbus," Smith adds. "He said, 'guys, there's this place we're going. I think it's going to be cool when we get there. I don't know how long it's going to take us to get there so kiss your wives goodbye because I'm not sure we're coming back.' Those guys had to have some faith."

Smith's observations struck me as spot-on. They point to some of the common pitfalls that cause other dealers to fall off the road to reinvention. I asked Smith and Hardman to share the lessons they learned from their first attempt at reinventing their used vehicle operations and how they've applied them to achieve success the second time around.

They offered seven key take-aways:

- **Disciplined, data-backed sourcing of used vehicles.** Hardman says the dealership abandoned what he calls "the force," which previously guided used vehicle acquisitions. "We'd go to auctions and say, 'we do great with those' and 'boy these are good sellers,'" Hardman says. Now, there's a keen focus on finding cars with high demand and interest and low market days supply. "It takes significantly more buying discipline," Smith says.

  This discipline occurs every night as an acquisition specialist scours available auctions to find cars that fit the dealership's buy list recommendations and purchase parameters. Each morning Hardman uses the list to guide auction acquisitions. The effort's mostly online—a nod to efficiency and the need to cast a wider net to get the "right" cars.

  "We can look at a lot more cars and the kind of cars we want," Hardman says. "We buy cars from all over the country."

- **More realistic, market-based pricing right out of the gate.** During the initial road to reinvention effort, Hardman says the dealership recognized the need to make their used vehicles more price-competitive to attract buyers. They applied a smaller mark-up, pricing cars to what they considered "the market."

  Even so, "our asking prices were 20 percent to 30 percent higher than they should have been," Hardman says. "We still priced them to the moon."

  Now, "we take each individual car on its own," he says. "If it's a car with a 90-day market days supply, we're not going to price it at 100 percent of market. The only way that car will perform better than 90 days is to sell it for less than 100 percent of the market."

  "Market days supply doesn't tell me how fast my cars will turn. It tells me how fast everybody else's cars will turn," Smith says. "If it's a low days supply car, it will tolerate a higher price. If it's a higher days supply car, you better start that thing on the money and be willing to go below the money."

- **Daily focus on each used car's destiny.** Brandon Smith, W.C.'s younger brother and partner in the dealership, meets with Hardman and body shop and service managers at 8:45 each morning. The goal: Discuss the progress on each car, from its status on the ground (in transit, reconditioning, detailing, etc.) and online (its photographs, pricing, descriptions, etc.).

"We didn't have the interest in getting those cars done quickly that we do now," Brandon Smith says. "In our body shop, for example, we used to take four or five days to get rid of the blemishes that every used car seems to have. Now, it's less than an hour and we know what it'll take to do the job and make the decision that day."

Hardman says this emphasis on reconditioning turn-time and the online presentation of each vehicle flowed from fully realizing time is money in today's Internet-driven environment. "We've taken it to a more extreme level because we realized one day makes a difference," he says. This includes Hardman spending significant time to track the feeds between systems that capture, post and syndicate used vehicle inventory listings to Monument's website and third-party classified sites like AutoTrader.com and Cars.com—and pushing vendors to do better.

"I knew nothing about all that stuff," Hardman says. "For some reason, I took on the task. I'm glad I did. I learned a lot. If dealers knew how long it took to get a car on a third party site, they'd fall out of their chairs. I fell out of mine for 60 days straight."

- **Top-down commitment and collaboration.** It took the Smiths and Hardman some time to educate their sales teams about the benefits of velocity management principles. Initially, they only saw the dip in front-end gross profits. They missed the larger, more paycheck-positive cumulative effect of selling more cars.

"Salespeople would say, 'we don't make money on the deals anymore,'" Hardman says. "We'd sit down and say, 'let's look at that.' Before you sold eight cars and made $X. Now you're selling 14. You don't make as much per car, but you're making more money than before. And, you don't have to go out there and justify why we're asking for the moon on a car. Instead of running from price, we're running to price."

"We had our plan and if we ran into a sticking point, we said, 'let's eliminate that obstacle,'" W.C. Smith says. "You've got to take it a day at a time and build confidence. You start with the big picture and then drill down."

- **Recognition of early wins.** One of the promises of velocity management is that the adoption of realistic, market-based pricing will generate more in-store traffic and sales. As this occurred at Monument, it became a teaching opportunity.

"You'll have small wins," Hardman says. "You'll list a car and someone from Kansas or Austin or Miami or Nigeria will call. You start being able to jump on those opportunities to educate your people. Why did those people come here? Under the old school way, we would not have sold that car. With the new school way, we're being noticed all over the country."

- **Occasional group therapy.** Hardman and Smith are quick to note their time on the road to reinvention tested their resolve more than once. "W.C.'s father is involved in the dealership and there would be times he would look at something and ask, 'are we going down the right path?' I would turn to W.C. and ask, 'how are you feeling.' He'd ask me the same question. You go on this emotional rollercoaster and managers feel it, too. You need to be prepared for that."

- **Planned, incremental growth.** In the summer of 2012, the Monument team has plans for additional growth in the dealership's used vehicle sales volumes. But they'll exercise the same careful planning and execution they've undertaken at other stages on their road to reinvention.

"There are some opportunities we'd have if we had a faster pace," Hardman says. "But it's not our style as a dealership. Our approach is to build something solid and then go for more growth. We hire people as needed to fill those positions and then take our next step."

I've highlighted Monument's story because it's chock-full of lessons for aspiring velocity dealers. It also underscores why the adoption of velocity principles and the road to reinvention really is like a "new religion" for dealers. It's daunting, all-encompassing, exciting and rewarding—all at the same time.

To my friends at Monument: Thank you. Good luck. Amen.

REDEFINING A "GOOD JOB" IN USED VEHICLES

I'll often ask dealers how they define a "good job" in their used vehicle operations.

Typically, the answer relates to a previous monthly sales record. Example: If a dealership's best monthly tally of used vehicle sales is 125, that number equals a "good job."

In today's more competitive marketplace, I believe dealers need to use a more comprehensive assessment of performance to determine if their used vehicle department is performing to its peak.

To be sure, sales volumes matter. But these tallies, in and of themselves, only reflect past performance.

They do not necessarily indicate whether a dealer is maximizing penetration in the current market, nor do they probe what a dealer's future market potential might look like.

To address this, I offer the following three components that dealers should use to redefine what they consider to be a "good job" in their used vehicle departments:

1. **Your market share:** This can be a difficult number to pin down. On the new vehicle side, manufacturers determine a dealer's market share in different ways. Some use the factory's national market share to benchmark a dealer's performance, others focus more on a dealer's designated market area (DMA) performance to determine market share. On top of that, factories calculate and credit out-of-market-area sales differently—sometimes they count toward a dealer's market share performance, other times they don't.

   Market share for used vehicles is arguably even more difficult to calculate—and a reason many dealers have not historically given it much attention.

   Joe Herman, COO of the 14-store Kuni Automotive Group, says that while a "good job" can be elusive to clearly define in terms of market share, it's very essential to look to future potential rather than the best, prior results.

"There's not a common way to calculate used vehicle market share," says dealer Keith Kocourek of Kocourek Chevrolet, Wausau, Wis. "Very few dealers look at that. We actually have 55 percent of our market. To us, that's a pretty good job. But some dealers in Dallas or Houston are doing 7 percent or 10 percent and they consider that a good job."

Kocourek and other velocity dealers don't let the difficulty of calculating their market share thwart the assessment of where they stand as used vehicle retailers and how they set sales volume goals for their stores.

At a minimum, this calculation should include an evaluation of used vehicle registrations and an analysis of the makes/models in specific vehicle segments to provide a baseline market share measurement. From there, velocity dealers will set their goals for increased sales and growth. While this calculation and goal-setting may not be perfect, it's an important and informed starting point for determining a "good job" in used vehicles.

"There's a sweet spot for every store in every market," Kocourek says. "For my stores, the sweet spot is 100-115 cars. At that point, we've saturated the market and pulled all the costs out of the system. We've found anything above that is just not as profitable. When we get there, I go out and buy another store."

"We constantly ask our dealerships, 'How much further can we go? What are the limits of our ultimate potential?'" Herman says. This mindset has helped propel "what was already good same-store used car performance to 23-plus percent growth in used vehicle sales for each of the past two years—a 52 percent overall improvement".

Herman says. "You won't really know what the ultimate potential is until you constantly push to find out."

2. **Your inventory turn rate.** Historically, dealers have lacked the technology and tools necessary to fully manage and maximize the return on investment (ROI) they can achieve from their used vehicle inventories. When I was a dealer, we set our inventory levels to satisfy three months' worth of sales (e.g., a 90-day supply). This approach meant that, on average, we would turn our inventory seven to eight times a year. Back then, this was a "good job" in our used vehicle department.

Since then, however, inventory management technology and tools have improved, and dealers have a keener understanding that turning your inventory faster means better ROI.

Today, a "good job" in used vehicles for velocity dealers means turning their inventories a minimum of 12 times a year. As we've noted in past chapters, some velocity dealers are able to more than double this rate, to 25 times a year.

The key is to manage inventory turns in tandem with goals for increased sales and market share—and watch for the telltale signs of an imbalance. "We know if we stock another 20 cars beyond the 'sweet spot' at our Chevy store, the turn goes down," Kocourek says. "It's another step in the road you have to manage."

On the plus side, the higher rates of inventory turn help velocity dealers maintain fresh inventories, maximize their front-end gross profit potential and minimize the risk of aged units.

3. **Your ROI/profitability:** Used vehicle consultant Tommy Gibbs of Tommy Gibbs and Associates, Treasure Island, FL., encourages dealers to keep a tally of the ROI status of every vehicle in their inventories. He recommends they strive to achieve ROI of 110 percent to 120 percent—roughly the same ROI an investor might seek—for their vehicles.

The ROI calculation includes the costs of a car (acquisition plus reconditioning), its front-end gross profit, its days in your inventory and your annual inventory turn rate. Gibbs says the calculation helps dealers recognize that they make less money (particularly on more expensive cars) the longer the vehicles remain in their inventories.

I like Gibbs' approach to determining the ROI for individual used vehicles. Dealers who seek consistent ROI improvement on every car will be doing a "good job" in used vehicles.

I also believe that a "good job" in used vehicles should measure the ROI and profitability a used vehicle department generates for the entire dealership. To be sure, dealers can intuitively see how velocity-driven used vehicle operations light up parts, service, F&I and sales departments. But I've found it's difficult to evaluate dealership financial statements and derive ROI benchmarks that would detail the cross-departmental gains in ROI and profitability that can be attributed to used vehicle operations and be meaningful for all dealers.

I've turned this difficulty into a personal directive: In the coming months, I will be working with velocity dealers to develop these broader, dealership-wide benchmarks and share them through my blog and other writings. Stay tuned.

In the meantime, dealers should recognize that this redefinition of a "good job" in used vehicles is like a three-legged stool: Each component must carry its share of the weight and work in tandem with the others for the used vehicle department to reach its fullest potential.

Four Cornerstones of "Maximum Velocity"

Not long after dealers embark on the road to reinvention and earnestly adopt velocity principles in used vehicles, some dealers will ask a question: "How high can I take this thing?"

I love this question. It's the mark of a dealer who has successfully traveled the road to reinvention in used vehicles. It's the sign of an entrepreneur who's hungry for more. It's a testimony to the caution and wisdom gained while making velocity management principles consistently work at a dealership. It signals a mind that is curious to keep pace with the fast-changing automotive retail marketplace.

Unfortunately, the answer to this question is, "It depends."

I know that's not a satisfying response, but it's a reality. Why? Because every dealer is different, and every dealership reflects its owner's personality and preferences.

Some dealers use velocity management principles to "own" their local used vehicle markets; others just want a bigger piece of their local pie. Beyond that, velocity management itself is still relatively nascent. It's only been widely adopted as a best practice for managing used vehicles in the past five years. To put it bluntly, the Velocity Method of Management™ is still evolving.

But while there is no clear-cut answer to the "how high can I take this thing?" question, there are key cornerstones that I believe must be in place for dealers to reach maximum velocity.

Cornerstone 1: Stair-step your growth. This goes hand-in-hand with the assessment of a dealership's market share potential noted in the last chapter. As velocity dealers ponder what maximum velocity means for their stores, they should recognize that incremental growth requires the capacity to handle it.

For example, dealer Steven Risso of Teddy Nissan in New York City has applied velocity principles to achieve 130 used vehicle sales each month; 90 percent of those are Nissan-built units.

"If I'm doing nearly 130 Nissans a month, what is my potential?," Risso asks. "How many more cars could I sell if I went after all the good used cars that sell? I think about that all the time. It's like a big piece of cake. Where should I take the first bite?"

Risso hasn't made the leap because he understands it would require additional reinvention to his processes for acquisition, reconditioning and sales.

"In some ways, I'm scared of the potential, to tell you the truth," Risso says. "I see what might be the next big opportunity in higher-mileage, older cars. But I've got to figure out a way to acquire and service them correctly first."

Cornerstone 2: Maximize efficiencies. In prior chapters, we've examined how velocity dealers have increased efficiencies in used vehicle acquisition, reconditioning, merchandising and sales. It should be clear to readers that it's essential to achieve these efficiencies before a store can reach maximum velocity—and that new and emerging technology and tools are an essential part of the efficiency equation.

At Vancouver, Wash.-based Kuni Automotive, for example, COO Joe Herman says the group has spent the past 30 months identifying best-in-class vendors for customer relationship management, mystery shopping, website development, F&I,

inventory management, service process management, and more.

"We've installed all of these systems in every Kuni store," Herman says. "We train on them regularly and we make a commitment to ourselves for each one of us to become Power Users."

This efficiency-oriented initiative ensures standard processes and metrics across the Western US, geographically diverse dealership group. "We all use the same weapons," Herman says. "We have the same metrics to compare our stores, and to keep focus on raising the level of our game."

Cornerstone 3: Embrace change. Dealer W.C. Smith of Monument Chevrolet in Pasadena, Texas, is 33 years old. He notes: "The business has changed more in the last five years than it has from the time my grandfather ran this store and I grew up in the business in the early '90s."

I think most dealers would agree, and they'd concur that the next few years will bring even more change. This evolutionary environment means change—and reinvention—will be constant companions for dealers who seek maximum velocity.

"The business model has become one that's constantly moving," dealer Keith Kocourek of Kocourek Chevrolet, Wausau, Wis., says. "But it's easier to manage because you have the metrics to do it."

Cornerstone 4: Create a sustainable system. I'm reminded of the words my good friend Russ Wallace used to share as I visited with him at the Bill Marsh Auto Group in Traverse City, Mich. I was always struck by how much time and energy he spent coaching and teaching other members of the Marsh team, irrespective of their role in the group.

"Dale, this isn't about me or just selling more used cars. This is about changing the way we do business to meet today's market and creating a system that will last long after I'm gone."

It chokes me up to realize how prophetic Russ' statement has become. But since his death in June 2011, the Marsh group has carried on with great success—following the paths and processes Russ engineered as he helped lead them down the road to reinvention.

This same mentality has guided velocity dealers like Kocourek and Herman as they've begun to pursue maximum velocity at their organizations.

"It's interesting," Kocourek says. "Before velocity, we all banked on a used car manager to know all this stuff and do it. You hung your hat on that guy.

"Now, I want to run my business based on metrics and process and I want to say, 'Larry you have this job,' and 'Ben, you have that job.' Then I can cross-train and switch those guys around," he says. "I don't want a situation where once a guy is gone, the whole thing blows up."

In addition to the "how high can I take this thing?" question, velocity dealers also ask me, "what happens if every dealer drinks the velocity Kool-Aid?" The answer to this question is similar, but slightly different than the first question. See the book's Postscript for my response.

REINVENTION IN ACTION: AN INTERNET-FOCUSED SALES STRUCTURE

In 2007, Joe Castle made a deal with his father.

The particulars: Castle, then 27, would take over the family's Chicago-area Buick, Pontiac, GMC and Chevrolet dealerships if he could successfully turn around their money-losing performance in six months.

"My father had called me one day and said, 'Joe, I'm going to sell the Chevy store. It's losing its butt. You've been doing good at the Buick store and it's turning around. Let's just focus on that store," Castle recalls.

"I got in my car and flew right over to the Chevy store," he says. "I sat down and said, 'Listen. I see the structure we have to use to become an Internet-focused dealership. I can turn this store around and make it profitable. Give me six months, and if I'm successful, I'll buy out both stores.

"But I want no interference. I want to be able to do what I have to do, and I'm going to have to clean house."

Castle's father approved the deal. And so began the reinvention of Castle's dealerships into stores that were principally and primarily focused on capturing more online new and used vehicle customers.

Castle's confidence came from early successes he'd seen reshaping the online merchandising and sales efforts at the family's Buick, Pontiac, GMC store. He had adopted velocity principles in its used vehicle department and invested more in listing his cars on classified sites like AutoTrader.com and Cars.com. The effort resulted in an increase of 20 to 30 monthly sales.

But Castle knew he could do better. While he'd achieved some success, the experience had also brought him head-to-head with traditional dealership people and processes that impeded his progress.

First, Castle recognized his growth would be limited by the capacity of his store's designated Internet managers. At the time, these salespeople were largely separate from the rest of the show-room team. Nearly all of the incremental sales gains came from these people.

Even worse, while his Internet managers were closing more deals, the rest of the traditional showroom sales staff "was looking out the window, waiting for an act of God to bring them a car deal," says Robert Politza, a former F&I manager whom Castle promoted to general manager to help over-see the turnaround efforts at both dealerships. "The Internet managers had all the action because all the action is on the Internet."

"That's when Bob and I started marking up a whiteboard and realized the whole structure of the traditional dealership is wrong," Castle says. "We needed to change our organization to get maximum results and structure our processes around the tech-nology and tools that help us capture and retain today's Internet customers. We've basically applied velocity principles everywhere in the dealership."

The results at the Castle stores are impressive: In three months, he turned a profit at the Chevrolet store, which had been losing money, sometimes as much as $100,000 a month, for more than a year. Since those early days, new/used vehicle sales have increased 200 percent (currently 130 new/200 used at the Chevrolet store). The average age of used vehicles at both stores is 23 days. Gross profits in fixed operations have increased five-fold. The stores are achieving record net profits.

"If a dealer wants to get back to the '80s when he was making $1 million or $2 million in net profit every year, and he's getting a true ROI out of the dealership as he should be, it's still there right in front of him," Castle says. "I don't care about what the news says. There is still that kind of net profit in a dealership to be made. The problem for many dealers is converting from a traditional structure to a more digitally focused structure."

The thinking behind Castle's reinvention effort is strikingly sophisticated yet simple: If I apply market-based velocity principles to maximize the appeal of my new and used vehicles and attract more customers, my dealership sales structure and processes need to be aligned to efficiently capture, manage and sell these online customers. Similarly, as this structural realignment occurs in sales, it must extend to fixed operations to maximize velocity, return on investment (ROI) and profitability throughout the dealership.

This reinvention required rethinking the roles and responsibilities of Internet managers, sales managers and used vehicle managers. It included redrawing the dealership's front-end organization chart (see diagram, next page). Further, it required changing dealership pay plans and processes to ensure they were attuned to achieve Castle's goals for increased velocity and volume of vehicle sales.

This reinvention wasn't easy.

New Dealership Org. Chart

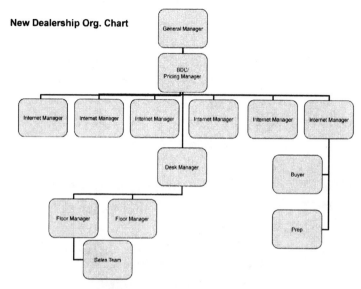

Castle estimates roughly 60 percent of the sales personnel left or didn't thrive in the new environment. Not everyone liked the new model and its requirement that they adapt to a new way of doing business and earning their paychecks.

"The traditional ways are kind of hard to kill," Politza says. "A lot of our people had been in the business a long time."

'You might lose some loyal soldiers in this transition," Castle adds. "But some people got promoted and managers who left came back."

In my second book, I shared the outline for what I considered a more efficient, Internet-focused sales department structure. Broadly, I encouraged dealers to collapse their new, used and Internet sales teams into a single organization to maximize efficiencies, lower costs and create the potential for maximum velocity in used vehicle departments and beyond.

Castle's model follows this sketch. His interpretation is unique and works well for his dealerships. I share it here not because it offers an end-all, be-all approach for other velocity- and reinvention-minded dealers. Rather, it illuminates a viable, directionally correct framework to help other dealers rethink and reinvent how they manage the "blocking and tackling" of velocity principles in their sales departments.

As Castle and Politza implemented their digitally focused dealership structure, they kept a clear eye focused on barriers to their goals for maximum velocity, ROI and profitability. When they encountered these barriers, they addressed them. The following are four beneficial outcomes of their concerted efforts:

A clearer accounting of customer inquiries and leads. Previously, Castle's sales team would handle incoming phone calls, and separate Internet managers would handle e-mail and other leads that originated online.

The problem: Salespeople didn't always properly track and follow-up with call-in customers, and Internet managers would "cherry-pick" leads—in part because their standalone positions in the sales department meant they handled all aspects of a deal, leaving insufficient time to fully work the pool of incoming opportunities.

"The traditional structure doesn't fit the flow of the customers and their needs," Castle says. "The customers are all online. They want more and more information. If you have Internet managers handling these customers, answering their questions and getting financing information, it caps your momentum. They'll cherry-pick the best leads and leave the rest.

"The traditional structure also creates communication barriers. The Internet managers are usually off to the side and not really connected to sales managers," he says. "And when customers who've done 80 percent of their homework online just walk in, the sales guy or the F&I guy is opening them up from scratch and probably losing them."

Now, Castle routes all incoming customer queries to a centralized business development center (BDC). There, the new "Internet managers" capture customer information, answer questions, assess financing and other needs and set appointments. In turn, they work with sales desk and floor managers to prep salespeople (what Castle calls "customer care representatives") for appointments on new and used vehicles.

"They just drive traffic to my dealerships," he says. "My sales consultants become product specialists and delivery coordinators."

This structure has given Castle a better view of the full extent of customer interest and the effectiveness of his investments in online advertising and merchandising.

"I used to think I got 50 phone calls and leads a month from AutoTrader.com and Cars.com," he says. "Overnight, it quadrupled and I knew how many I was really getting. Right away, I realized that even if our closing rates stayed the same, we would have an increase in sales."

A better customer experience. Castle says the new structure has eliminated a scenario that remains too common at many dealerships: A customer walks into the showroom and the salesperson has little or no idea of how much they've already shopped the dealership online or whether they've contacted the store prior to coming in.

The dealership's new structure and its CRM and inventory management tools give floor managers and salespeople the ability to quickly identify a customer's previous inquiries or visits. If it's truly a fresh 'up,' they are now trained (and held accountable) to capture the customer's information and focus on the specific vehicle(s) that fits the customer's interests and needs.

"The traditional structure creates communication barriers," Castle says. "Our new structure ensures we complete the circle with every customer from the initial appointment and sale to future visits in service. When a customer comes through the door, everybody knows what the BDC told that customer, so there's no disruption in the communication stream."

Lower costs. As they adopted the new structure and processes, Castle and Politza looked for cost and operational efficiencies. They recognized the new structure allowed them to parse responsibilities that previously rested on the shoulders of higher-paid used vehicle and general sales managers.

"We've broken up the jobs into pieces," Politza says. "We have lower-paid people doing the jobs rather than one guy trying to do it all and not doing it well. You may have 20 percent more people but your overall dollar expense is similar or less. You have a lot of capacity to handle the high volumes."

The process- and task-oriented nature of these positions means salespeople are more productive. At Castle's stores, the average salesperson sells 15 cars a month compared to other GM dealers in the region where the average is 10. "That's a 50 percent increase in productivity per person," Politza says.

To be sure, the changes in roles and responsibilities, as well as the focus on increasing the velocity and volume of sales, required significant changes in the pay plans for sales department personnel. The key: Eliminate nearly all average gross profit-related incentives and point pay plans toward the ultimate goal—selling more cars.

For example, in the BDC, Internet managers earn roughly 40 percent of their pay from appointments and gross profits from the sales generated from customers they managed. In sales, the customer care representatives' pay plans blend a base salary with bonuses based on volume (75 percent) and customer satisfaction index (CSI) ratings (25 percent).

"We're getting a lot more out of our people," Politza says. "The average gross per salesperson is almost double the traditional store, even with the highs and lows of the business. And, I don't get payroll complaints on Friday with questions about why a commission wasn't what the salesperson expected. All of that ended. We're still evolving this, but it's working better than before."

In addition to changes in pay plans and positions, Castle credits the model's lower operational costs to the near-elimination of traditional advertising. "I was spending $40,000 to $50,000 a month on traditional advertising, or about $400 to $500 a car," he says. "I cut it down to $10,000 and put the money into the classified sites and my website. I'm down to about $100 per car."

Improved ROI/profitability in fixed operations. As Castle and Politza aligned their sales department structure to increase the volume of their new/used vehicle sales, they recognized the opportunity to extend velocity principles into their fixed operations department.

"It's an even bigger challenge in fixed operations, but it has a higher return on investment," Politza says. "You'll find all of the same roadblocks you might in sales. Shops tend to manage themselves to where they want to be. They may believe they can only handle 20 appointments a day when there's enough calls to do 50. They'll spread things out and schedule the customers later. It slows everything down."

To address the bottleneck, Castle and Politza worked with their fixed operations director to increase capacity.

"The first task is changing the attitude of the service manager and fixed ops director to understand that the status quo doesn't work," Politza says. "It goes all the way down to the simplest thing like not having two stalls per technician. Now we have two guys in those stalls. If they can't finish a repair, they pull the car down and start on another one. The stalls are always producing."

In addition, the dealership's BDC now handles appointments for the service departments to maximize the amount of customer pay work.

Politza notes the dealership's gross profits in fixed operations has increased 200 percent and they've added a second shift to accommodate the additional customer pay work, as well as the higher volume of internal work that flows from reconditioning more used vehicles.

"The extra shift was a leap of faith at first, but the return on investment has proven to be worth it," he says.

I asked Castle what his father, who's since retired to Florida, thinks of the uptick in business and profitability at his stores.

"He'll look at me and say, 'whatever you're doing, just keep doing it. I have no idea what's going on. It's not what I'm accustomed to, but just keep sending me my checks,'" Castle says with a laugh. "He thinks it's insane and that we're giving away cars. But he loves it. He knows our stores were taking a beating and now he can have a little bit of pride as he retires."

The "New Normal" Used Vehicle Marketplace

"It's going to be nice when the used vehicle business gets back to being normal."

I've heard this comment from a lot of dealers as they work to reinvent their used vehicle operations to maximize their return on investment (ROI) and profitability.

Most often, the dealers are optimistically looking forward to the day when the current up-tick in new vehicle sales will feed more used vehicles into the pipeline—easing the challenge of finding the "right" cars for their inventories and reducing the historically high wholesale prices of used cars.

For these dealers, I bring not-so-good news: The relief you're seeking from the market isn't likely to happen to the degree you'd like to see. For all intents and purposes, the dynamics that have made the used vehicle marketplace more challenging in recent years are, for the most part, here to stay.

There are three factors that contribute to what I would call the "new normal" for the used vehicle marketplace:

1. **High average wholesale values.** "Overall wholesale prices are high from a historic perspective," says Tom Webb, chief economist of Manheim. He notes that while wholesale values and prices are likely to soften, "they'll continue to be higher than what people have anticipated in the past."

   This assessment throws a little cold water on dealer expectations that wholesale values will decline and ease the competition between new vehicles and late model used vehicles. The days of acquiring late model used vehicles for 50 percent of the manufacturer's suggested retail price (MSRP) for comparable used units may well be gone.

   Webb attributes this "new normal" state of the wholesale marketplace to increased competition to acquire vehicles among dealers who have made used vehicles a higher priority. In addition, factories have been less aggressive with new vehicle incentives, lease buy-backs and the build-up of fleet cars in recent years. Typically, some of the largest declines in wholesale vehicle values occur as a result of factory programs shifting market supply and demand dynamics in used vehicles, Webb says.

"I don't think we'll see the industry go back to the ways of the past," he says. "If you're profitable at 13.5 million sales, why push it to 14 million or more? But sometimes factories do illogical things. We know that."

The key take-away for dealers: It will continue to be important to manage the average unit cost and composition of your used vehicle inventory to differentiate its value proposition from new vehicle offerings. It'll also be important to keep an eye on factory efforts to drive new vehicle sales and market share—and adjust inventories accordingly.

"When factories offer a $199/month lease deal on a new model, the monthly payment on a three-year-old car of the same make and model isn't even going to come close for a customer," Webb says.

2. **Ongoing margin compression.** As more dealers adopt market-focused retail pricing for their used vehicles, it's not uncommon to see vehicles and their price points "cluster" in a given market. This is an attribute of an efficient market—the market defines the "sweet spot" where retailers

and buyers typically transact for goods and services.

For dealers, this dynamic means greater vigilance in acquiring vehicles for the "right" money and "pricing for profitability, not profit" as these cars become retail units. It also means, as we've discussed in previous chapters, that dealers must actively address inefficiencies in their people and processes to maximize used vehicle ROI and profitability.

"You can see there's more aggressive and more astute pricing in the market," says dealer Mike Marsh of the Bill Marsh Auto Group, Traverse City, Mich. "Some dealers are very aggressive. We have to be more efficient. We have to be leaner, much more agile and quicker."

"Your margins are less than they once were," says Jack Anderson, used vehicle director for West Herr Automotive, Buffalo, N.Y. "There's a little bit of a flight to the bottom where the lowest price wins. We're working to hold our margin by decreasing negotiation and saving money as we buy cars to give us a competitive advantage."

3. **Consumer expectations for transparency.** It's no secret that today's buyers expect to find used cars "in the market" and "on the money" as they shop online. The growing number of dealers who have adopted market-based pricing strategies reflects this reality.

In time, however, consumer expectations for pricing transparency will grow—and more buyers will be less interested in negotiating deals. The rise of companies like TrueCar, which promises buyers the "best local price" and a "better buying experience," is fueling this movement.

This means that the "documentation as the new negotiation" we detailed in Chapter 21 will become more common in dealer showrooms. As we discussed, dealers who embrace transparency find it's just as profitable, if not more so, than the traditional "hold 'em and fold 'em"-style of selling cars.

"People will pay more to avoid the conflict on the showroom floor," says Mark Rikess, head of The Rikess Group, a Los Angeles firm that advises dealers on one-price selling and sales process transparency. "It's counter-intuitive for some dealers to realize that increased transparency adds value for buyers, which means less resistance to price."

"As more dealers offer relevant pricing, price is less of a factor," says Chad Lemieux, used car director for the Los Angeles-based, The Car Group. "When that happens, differential delivery becomes the key to success. That's where I'm putting my weight right now."

Lemieux's point underscores another aspect of the "new normal" in used vehicles: This marketplace is arguably more evolutionary and volatile than it's ever been. Dealers who are quickest to adapt will fare better than those who resist its ever-changing nature.

As I contemplate the "new normal," I'm reminded of an instructive quote from science fiction author and pioneer Isaac Asimov: "It is change, continuing change, inevitable change, that is the dominant factor in society today. No sensible decision can be made any longer without taking into account not only the world as it is, but the world as it will be."

A Peek Inside Dale's Crystal Ball

Every person has at least one characteristic that might be described as both a blessing and a curse.

For me, it's an inability to hold my tongue when I think I've got the right answer to a question, or I hear someone offer a point that doesn't make sense or seems flat-out wrong.

I was never a loud-mouth, know-it-all. My motivation isn't to simply hear my voice. Rather, I aim to shed light on a dark corner or offer clarity in murky waters. I try to be respectful when I offer my point of view.

I share this mini-confessional to provide the proper context for this Crystal Ball chapter. As I look ahead at the future of our industry, I see several things today's dealers won't like or want to hear. Even so, I'm compelled to share them for two reasons.

First, they offer a map for the as-yet unchartered territory that the road to reinvention will cross in the coming years. Second, I believe that dealers who prepare today for tomorrow's challenges will be far better positioned to meet them and maximize their return on investment (ROI) and profitability for their dealerships.

Perhaps the best news here is that much of what I view as future challenges for car dealers have already manifested themselves in the business today. In other words, the signs of what's to come are apparent to those who take the time to notice the clues and discern what they mean.

In this way, my Crystal Ball may be more like the magnifying glass Sherlock Holmes famously used to examine evidence and solve his cases. The following are the four future challenges that I've discerned from a careful read of today's business and what it portends in the coming years:

1. **The Rise of E-Commerce.** As a parent, I'm some-times frustrated that it's easier to reach my kids via a text message rather than talking to them directly on the phone. More than once I've been

told to "get over it" and "this is how we roll" as I've unsuccessfully tried to communicate with my kids in the manner I prefer.

The end result: I've adapted to "how they roll." The conversations I crave will come, but they're less frequent than the text and e-mail messages that have become staples of keeping in touch with my family. I've made this adjustment because my end goal—connecting with the people I love most—matters more than the medium I use to achieve it.

Increasingly, I believe dealers need to make the same adjustment as they think of ways to better serve tomorrow's customers. These buyers will be members of Gen Y, just like my kids.

Industry studies show that 60 percent of Gen Y buyers are reluctant to visit dealerships, and as many as 80 percent would prefer to avoid the F&I office altogether. In addition, they want an efficient and transparent sales process.

It's this backdrop that is pushing more vendors to offer dealers online technology and tools that aid the purchasing and financing of new and used vehicles. Already, some dealers report that they're selling more new vehicles sight-unseen to customers—and delivering them to customers who haven't visited the dealership.

"We're hearing more and more customers saying, 'I don't need to test drive the car. It's got four wheels. It looks cool. It synchs with my iPhone. I don't want to buy the car if it's broken but I don't care how it drives,'" says dealer Andrew DiFeo of Hyundai of St. Augustine, Fla. "I think this will still be a minority of customers but it's an indicator of where the business is going."

In Minneapolis, the Walser Auto Group has begun embracing this emerging breed of customer. In late summer of 2012, the 10-store group launched an "I'll Take It" online-buying program. It allows buyers to place a $500 deposit on a vehicle and complete the paperwork for a deal via e-mail and/or an online application.

"The program's built to be customer-centric," says Doug Sprinthall, director of vehicle operations at Walser. "The joke around here is that we're trying to do what really smart online retailers started doing in 1998.

"We asked ourselves, why not give customers another opportunity to interact with us in the way they want to?" he says. "We've got live chat. We've got all these different avenues people can use to communicate with us. Why not see if people would be interested in buying cars online?"

Sprinthall says Walser has already sold six vehicles (five used, one new) within the first four days of the "I'll Take It" program going live. Like DiFeo, he doesn't believe these customers will represent a majority of buyers in the near future, but the initial market response suggests the program will see greater traction.

Sprinthall says the "I'll Take It" program gives customers plenty of opportunities to back out of a deal if it doesn't feel right or a vehicle's appearance or condition doesn't meet expectations.

"It's designed not to trap customers. At every step, there's a way to stop the process and get a refund," Sprinthall says. "We asked, 'what would Amazon, Nordstrom's or Macy's do if someone bought something online and didn't like it?' They just take it back. That's the way you do it. That's the way every retail business works except the car business."

I like the way Sprinthall and the Walser team is thinking. The "I'll Take It" program is a perfect example of a dealership on the road to reinvention, seeking new ways to better serve customers.

Perhaps most important, Walser's program is a also big step toward a more e-commerce driven business model that I believe will become increasingly important for dealers to embrace in the not-too-distant future.

I asked Sprinthall why the Walser group appears more willing than other dealers to venture into this largely uncharted, buy-it-online territory.

"It's like the story of two guys walking in the woods and a bear approaches," he says. "One guy is putting on his sneakers and the other asks, 'Why are you doing that? You can't outrun a bear.' The other guy replies, 'I only have to out-run you.'"

My prediction: As each year passes, a greater number of dealers will adopt online-focused sales programs like the one Walser offers, allowing a greater portion of vehicle deals to occur online without the kind of in-store experience that has traditionally defined the car-buying process.

I recognize dealers are loath to hear this. Our business has traditionally been one where personalities, whether in sales, F&I or service, have made the difference with customers. I'm not suggesting this dynamic will go away completely, but I do believe dealers will see less need for as many people to handle vehicle transactions as they currently require.

Further, as we'll see below, there are other emerging realities of the business that may leave dealers no choice but to pursue the people and process efficiencies e-commerce appears to promise.

2. **Greater margin compression.** I see three challenges here—the first two of which relate to the partnerships between dealers and factories.

Challenge 1: Factory-driven facility upgrades. This has been growing as an industry hot-button, particularly as new vehicle sales have increased from their recession-era levels. Factories now want dealers to make good on facility programs they've resisted.

But "every dealer knows another dealer who got in trouble in the recession," says dealer-broker Mark Johnson of MD Johnson, Inc., Enumclaw, Wash. "Ninety-nine percent of the time the trouble had to do with over-building on the facility. There's a lot of sensitivity to real estate costs out there."

In early 2012, the National Automobile Dealers Association released a study that many dealers hoped would help underscore the reality they feel in their stores—a $1 million to $3 million upgrade doesn't pencil in today's retailing environment. Many dealers thought the study raised more questions than it answered, and the pressure on dealers to update or rebuild facilities continues.

Like so many consumers, dealers are still feeling the pain of the economic downturn. Their land and buildings have lost value, in some cases by as much as 30 percent. I haven't seen any economic forecasts that suggest the value of these real estate assets are increasing—in fact, they've become a significant bogey in buy/sell deals.

"There's a quantum change in the mentality of 20 percent to 30 percent of dealers who are acquiring stores," Johnson says. "We're dealing with buyers who, for the first time, won't buy the real estate. They feel like it's a dead-weight asset. They don't expect to get any capital growth from it."

While I don't have a dog in this fight, my emotions and instincts side with the dealers. I understand a factory's need to standardize the dealership experience with their brands, but I have an even greater respect for a dealer's latitude to truly operate as an entrepreneur. Put simply, the factory facility requirements, writ large, crimp the entrepreneurial nature of the business.

There are lawsuits currently underway that may ease pressure on dealers who have to satisfy factory facility requirements. But this won't change the underlying fundamentals of the situation: Many dealers currently own large, inefficient buildings on some of the most expensive ground in their local markets. And, there are few, if any, signs that these investments will appreciate in the next two to three years.

If I had my way, I would offer a better, more efficiency-minded blueprint for the next generation of dealerships (see image, next page). The concept: Locate the facilities on less-expensive real estate; build up instead of out, using less expensive materials; direct sales customer traffic into the showroom *before* they can walk your inventory (thank you, CarMax, for a great idea).

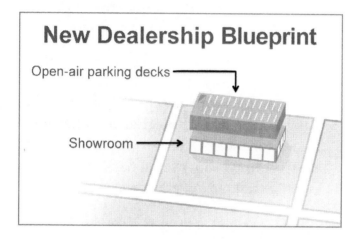

New Dealership Blueprint

Open-air parking decks

Showroom

This model would address the fact that a) dealership location matters less than it used to now that a store's front line is really online for most buyers; and b) dealers need less expansive inventories as they ramp up velocity principles in used vehicles and factories maintain more market-realistic new vehicle production levels.

"Dealers need to recognize that a store's website is far, far more important than its physical structure," says Joe Herman, COO of Kuni Automotive in Vancouver, Wash. "Dealers need to thoroughly understand how to utilize the web to improve their business. Locational focus limits a store's ultimate potential."

Challenge 2: Below-the-line monies: For much of the past decade, factories have been narrowing the margin between the manufacturer's suggested retail price (MSRP) and the invoice price on new vehicles. This has been done largely in the name of pricing transparency for consumers.

For dealers, this trend has narrowed the MSRP-to-invoice "spread" they've historically used to negotiate deals with customers. Now, in more highly competitive markets, discount-oriented dealers routinely use the formerly sacred (and mostly secret) factory "hold-back" money to negotiate transaction prices with customers.

This has not been a positive trend for dealers. Most will say the resulting compression on vehicle transaction prices and front-end gross profit in today's market is highly painful and unprecedented. This is why the new car department effectively functions as a "loss leader" at many dealerships.

Factories haven't been blind to these profitability pressures on dealers. Most now offer some type of performance-based incentive program that provides money for dealers who meet factory-set customer satisfaction, sales and, in some cases, facilities requirements.

I'm not sharing any industry secrets when I say dealers love, love, love the "below-the-line" money. For many dealers, it's a little bit like crack cocaine—once they're on it, they come back for more again and again.

At some dealerships, this "below-the-line" money has now become the difference between keeping the showroom doors open for business and boarding them up for good.

As I look ahead, I believe the "below-the-line" money will become even more problematic.

First, dealers will lose a little bit more of their autonomy as entrepreneurs. Dealers who have resisted factory facility upgrade requirements while accepting facility-related incentives have a problem. They would not appear to have much latitude to say "no" to factory expectations (an issue at play in the aforementioned lawsuits).

Second, "below-the-line" money will likely need to move "above the line" in today's environment. Some dealerships already use this money as they negotiate deals with customers. Others recognize the necessity of spreading it through the store—most often to ensure their people share in the rewards of selling cars and turning inventory. "You don't have that top bucket to pay your people off in the traditional fashion," Herman says.

Third, factories have the option to take the money away or change the "below-the-line" incentive program at any time. If I'm a dealer who's counting on $700/car in "below-the-line" money, and the factory reduces it to $450/car, I now have more than just a profitability problem.

Challenge 3: Business costs are going up, not down. I haven't heard of any dealership suppliers or vendors cutting prices. Factories aren't talking about increasing dealer margins. It's a far better bet that capital gains, property, income and other taxes and operating expenses will go up rather than down in the near future.

To me, the pressures of these rising costs further signal the need for the efficiency-and profitability-focused reinvention we've discussed throughout this book. It's simply not possible to rely on cost controls to ensure a viable and profitable future as a dealer.

3. **Increasing Consolidation:** The dealers who are most successful in the current environment have traveled the road to reinvention and achieved a greater degree of efficiency than their competitors. They have found faster, less-costly ways to sell more new and used vehicles. These are the dealers who are out buying stores from other dealers who, for whatever reason, have opted to throw in the towel.

"The typical buyer's story today is about an entrepreneur who wants to take the money his business has thrown off to create more wealth," Johnson says. "He wants to grow his business and acquire another deal that will add to his investment."

This dynamic only exacerbates the profitability problems for dealers who have not yet embarked on the road to reinvention in their dealerships. They now face bigger, leaner and more profitable competitors. In some cases, these consolidators can leverage their size and scale to directly affect market demand, supply, pricing and profitability.

Dealer Keith Kocourek of Kocourek Chevrolet, Wausau, Wisconsin, has leveraged his success in used vehicles to acquire more dealerships. Now, he's eyeing another market segment to drive his dealer group's ROI and profitability—the used vehicle market now controlled largely by independent dealerships.

"If I take that cost out of it and I'm competitive at that end of the market, where will a customer go?'" Koucourek asks. "Will they go to some place that sells five cars a month or one that sells 75 because of selection, quality and the return policy?"

I think we all know the answers to his questions.

4. **Increasing Convergence:** This goes well beyond the convergence of companies, like the acquisition of vAuto by AutoTrader.com. This type of convergence will continue in earnest as entrepreneurs develop technologies and tools that help

dealerships become more efficient and effective, and larger companies acquire them to leverage opportunities for growth and synergy.

The broader convergence I'm thinking about is occurring online—and it's a good, albeit challenging, development for dealers. Perhaps the most telltale signs of this convergence are occurring on dealership websites every day.

"In 2005, dealership sites were sixth on the list of sites automotive shoppers go to the most. In 2011, dealership sites were second," says Jason Ezell, CEO of Dataium, LLC., a Nashville-based company that tracks online traffic and trends. "Dealership sites have skyrocketed up the ranks."

Dataium's findings square with data from Google. "More people are going directly to dealer websites through search," says Peter Leto, a member of Google's Dealer JumpStart team. At the 2012 National Automobile Dealers Association convention, Leto noted a 31 percent year-over-year increase in search-driven traffic to dealership websites.

The Internet and search "used to be all about reach," Leto says. Now, "the Web is going local."

I call this the "Great Internet Give-Back:" Whereas in years past, dealers felt like the Internet was stealing away the business, it's now bringing customers back.

The key, of course, is recognizing and leveraging the role a dealer's website plays as a catcher's mitt for customers—no matter if they use a desktop computer, laptop or mobile device.

"At the end of the day, the No. 1 thing customers want when they hit the site is going to come down to inventory. That's never changed," says Kevin Frye, e-commerce director at Wyler Automotive, Cincinnati. "If you give customers the inventory and hit the financing and trade-in hot buttons, you'll be in good shape.

"We've switched to that model and have seen the highest dealership website conversions ever," he says. "It's about being transparent and giving them what they want. The reality of today's market is if you don't provide the information, and somebody else does, the customers will go there."

Dealer Andrew DiFeo of Hyundai of St. Augustine, Fla., also sees the "going local" trend as an opportunity. Today's vehicle shopper visits nearly 20 online sources during the car shopping process, according to industry stats. To DiFeo, this is a call to do more with his dealership websites and other online assets to "catch" these buyers before they go somewhere else.

"The shopping process seems inefficient," DiFeo says. "There has to be a better, more streamlined experience for online customers."

To me, the outcome of these online dynamics is pretty clear: E-commerce is coming to dealerships at a pace faster than we think. The dealers who will win big in this environment are those who reinvent the way they do business first—with more efficient, transparent Internet-driven processes and fewer in-person touch points.

As I noted above, each of these four future-focused challenges are, to varying degrees, with us today. This is the good news. They should represent familiar terrain along the road to reinvention we've been traveling throughout the book.

The bad news is that the road to reinvention isn't a cakewalk and, arguably, it never ends. To help dealers navigate this road, I've included 10 Road To Reinvention Commandments in the book's Epilogue.

It takes courage and will to venture down the road to reinvention. But I believe dealers who are earnest and honest about the journey will reap the rewards it delivers..

The Grateful Dead's "Ripple" offers a proper road-to-reinvention send-off:

> *There is a road. No simple highway.*
> *Between the dawn and the dark of night.*
> *And if you go, no one may follow.*
> *That path is for your steps alone.*

Epilogue: 10 Road to Reinvention Commandments

Throughout *Velocity Overdrive: The Road to Reinvention,* I've attempted to highlight the specific ways velocity dealers have reinvented people and processes in their used vehicle and other departments to maximize the return on investment (ROI) and profitability potential of their dealerships.

I've also tried to underscore how the road to reinvention requires dealers and their key managers to let go of traditional beliefs and leadership practices to ensure their velocity-driven goals fully materialize.

As we noted in Chapter 22, the road to reinvention really is like adopting a "new religion." The

following are what I would consider the 10 Road
to Reinvention Commandments to help guide
dealers toward converting their dealerships to the
more discipline- and efficiency-driven way of doing
business that today's used vehicle marketplace
requires.

1. **Let the market guide you.** It's no longer okay
   to trust the instinct or "golden gut" of a used
   vehicle manager to consistently make the correct decisions about the "right" cars, the "right"
   prices and the "right" exit strategy for every used
   vehicle in a given market. This isn't to suggest
   that good "car guy" instincts have no place in
   the day-to-day decision-making at dealerships.
   Rather, these instincts must be melded with
   market data and metrics to know if a decision to
   acquire, recondition, retail or wholesale a unit is
   the "right" one for the car, the dealership and the
   broader market.

2. **Understand the four critical inventory management metrics.** It takes time for the metrics or
   vehicle vital signs we reviewed in Chapter 2
   to truly sink in with managers and inventory
   acquisition specialists. The following recaps
   these metrics and includes benchmarks to
   help dealers deploy them to guide used vehicle
   decision-making:

   1. *Market Days Supply*: This measures the
      supply/demand characteristics of each car
      in a market. A high market days supply

means a unit faces greater competition from the same/similar cars available in a market. A lower market days supply means less competition. Dealers should use this metric to guide used vehicle acquisition and inform used vehicle pricing decisions. A benchmark: Strive to acquire vehicles with a market days supply of 70 or lower.

2. *Cost to Market:* This metric measures the "spread" between the costs of a vehicle and its prevailing retail price points. It can be measured in two ways:

   Acquisition Cost To Market: This measures the difference between the amount a dealer pays to acquire a vehicle and its prevailing retail price point. In general, velocity dealers aim to purchase vehicles at auction or trade-in with an average cost to market range of 78 percent to 80 percent.

   Total Cost to Market: This measures the "wrap-up" costs of acquiring and reconditioning a vehicle, as well as the addition of a pack, against its prevailing retail price point. The best-performing velocity dealers achieve an average 84 percent "total cost to market" on their retail-ready vehicles. These dealers strive to acquire vehicles at a 78 percent to 80 percent cost to market average, and

work hard to keep the costs of reconditioning and any pack amounts from
4 percent to 6 percent of the vehicle's
prevailing retail price.

Note: These benchmarks are simply averages. Dealers will see attractive vehicles with low market days
supply and a cost to market metric that exceeds
the benchmarks. As we noted in Chapters 2 and 16,
velocity dealers will acquire these vehicles because
a) the market days supply metric indicates a market-
desirable, fast-selling unit that will aid their inventory
turn goals and b) they can carefully manage acquisition and reconditioning/pack costs to ensure a
competitive retail asking price and sufficient "spread"
to meet ROI and profitability targets.

3. *Price to Market:* This metric measures the
   relationship between the asking price on a
   vehicle and the average retail price for the
   same/similar units available in a market.
   The metric is essential to ensure each used
   vehicle's asking price is "in the market"
   and "on the money." This will maximize
   its appeal with price-smart buyers. Velocity dealers use this metric as they set initial
   asking prices for vehicles and adjust them
   as they age. As noted in Chapter 2, the following is a common strategy for applying
   the price to market metric across inventory
   "age buckets:" 0-15 days, 96 percent price
   to market; 15-30 days, 93 percent; 30-45
   days, 89 percent.

Note: This strategy is only a guide. Some vehicles, due to scarcity or significant demand, "stand tall" in a market. In these cases, the car may warrant initial asking prices at or above 100 percent price to market given the unit's strong potential market appeal.

4. *Average age of inventory.* There are two key benefits that flow from paying close attention to the average age of your used vehicle inventory. First, the used vehicle department will see a higher level of profitability as it strives to maintain at least 50 percent of the inventory under 30 days of age. This follows the age-old axiom that "fresh cars hold the most gross." Second, this inventory management imperative minimizes the profit-draining risks of aging inventory and wholesale losses. Some velocity dealers have gone into "overdrive" when it comes to inventory age: They maintain 65 percent or more of their inventory under 30 days of age.

3. **Define and execute a used vehicle investment strategy.** In today's market, it's no longer okay to simply "sell used cars" and hope to maximize your ROI and profitability. The solution: A defined inventory investment strategy that blends and balances a dealer's strengths as a retailer with the local market. As we discussed in Chapter 6, dealers should approach their investment strategy like a financial manager.

The first step is defining the best type or class of investments (e.g., vehicle segments like compact, sedan, SUV, truck) for their dealerships and local market. These are the equivalent of the stocks, bonds or real estate investments financial managers would suggest for clients.

Second, dealers should determine how much to invest in each vehicle segment or strategic "bucket." This entails determining the number of cars (e.g., the dealership days supply) and the price tiers within each "bucket" that offer the best opportunity to maximize inventory turn, sales and ROI.

It's important to recognize that the investment strategy can and should be different for individual dealerships and markets.

Dealers who have built a reputation as the go-to place to buy trucks should leverage this brand identity as they develop their strategy. The same goes for dealers who specialize in high-line or "value" vehicles.

Today's technology and tools help dealers mine market data to create an investment strategy that plays to their individual strengths as retailers and helps them identify opportunities they have yet to explore. These inventory management tools also help dealers execute their strategy.

For example, vAuto's Provision system tells dealers the specific vehicles they need to acquire or sell to fit their inventory investment strategy.

A final point: A good investment strategy, whether it's in used vehicles or high finance, is never static. Dealers should revisit their used vehicle inventory investment strategy at least once a quarter to account for seasonal changes and other market factors (e.g., volatility from gas prices or economic turmoil) that will inevitably occur.

4. **Trust technology, market metrics to guide used vehicle decision-making.** "That computer doesn't know ****." I don't hear this as much as I used to, but there are still dealers and used vehicle managers who resist believing that technology and market metrics can help them become better, more profitable used vehicle retailers.

Best I can tell, the principal source of this resistance is a fear of accountability. Poor appraisal, buying or pricing decisions are sure to see the light of day as dealers diligently manage and monitor their inventory vital signs and metrics on a daily basis.

To me, this degree of technology-aided accountability is a huge opportunity. It gives dealers the ability to spot and fix mistakes rather than repeat them over and over again. It provides an analytical pathway to train people and re-think processes when your road to reinvention hits a roadblock.

As indicated above, trust in technology and market metrics should complement, not replace, well-honed "car guy" instincts. This combination continues to prove an ROI and profitability winner for velocity dealers. If resistance to the use of technology and reliance on market metrics becomes problematic, dealers need to find a work-around or different people to do the job.

5. **Adopt a "total gross" mindset.** In Chapter 9, we discussed why a "fixation on average front-end gross" is problematic for dealers in today's market.

   It tends to mask and mute the "wheel of fortune" benefits a dealer can generate beyond the used vehicle department in sales, parts, service and F&I. Further, the fixation on front-end gross too often veils other sins, such as letting vehicles age to achieve maximum front-end gross profit, that diminish a dealership's overall performance.

   Velocity dealers recognize that as they shift their focus to "total gross," they will, by definition, identify and address the people and process inefficiencies that slow their road to reinvention progress and ability to maximize ROI and profitability.

I should also add that the "total gross" mindset requires reinventing pay plans to compensate managers, sales associates and others in a manner that focuses less on average front-end gross and more on their individual and collective contributions that drive dealership-wide velocity of your sales and overall profitability (Chapter 21).

6. **Make improved efficiencies mission-critical.** In the book's introduction, I noted how the road to reinvention is really about a "race to efficiencies" for dealers. Throughout the book, we've examined efficiency-focused reinvention in used vehicle acquisitions via auctions (Chapters 7 and 12) and appraisals (Chapters 10 and 11), reconditioning (Chapters 14 and 15), pricing (Chapters 16), online merchandising (Chapter 18), desking and sales (Chapter 21).

There are three key reasons why greater efficiencies translates to greater success in today's retail marketplace.

First, time is money in today's more competitive, margin-compressed and highly volatile market. Velocity dealers recognize any delays in the acquisition, reconditioning, merchandising and sales of a vehicle translate to lost gross profit potential.

Second, increased efficiencies mean dealers are better able to consistently sell fresh cars fast, which drives velocity management's "turn and earn" benefits and reduces the risks of wholesale losses.

Third, the emphasis on increased efficiencies breeds a shared sense of discipline, purpose and urgency in a dealership. Even someone like me who can't see can readily sense when a dealership's really humming—the energy and enthusiasm are palpable. Efficiency-focused dealers make the can-do, get-on-the-stick attitude that typically closes a Saturday morning sales meeting part of the daily culture at their dealership.

7. **Maximize your online merchandising.** In my second book, I urged dealers to hire a "pixel professional"—someone who understands online buyers and the way they use search engines, classified sites, factory/dealership websites and social media to shop for and purchase cars. This recommendation follows recognition that today's car business is an Internet-driven business, and dealers need to compete more effectively online.

The "pixel professional" knows how to efficiently complete/update compelling, robust vehicle listings. This person knows how to read and react to the online merchandising metrics (namely, SRP/VDP conversions) that detail the ongoing market appeal and performance of every car.

Many of the velocity dealers noted in this book have hired "pixel professionals" and they are now a key factor behind the ROI and profitability gains they've achieved in their dealerships. At some stores, these individuals have replaced traditional used vehicle managers. They use velocity metrics and principles, and their online know-how, to acquire and merchandise vehicles.

A prediction: The role of the "pixel professional" will become even more important as our business increasingly becomes more e-commerce-driven and a greater share of vehicle sales transactions will occur online.

8. **Re-think the way you "win" with customers.** If we're honest with ourselves, the car deals we used to regard as a "win" for the dealership often left customers with a bad taste. You know what I'm talking about—the high-five-inducing, home run-gross deals that took advantage of customers who lacked sufficient smarts to push back effectively against the closers who manned our sales desks.

Today's customers, however, are different. They are smarter about the elements of a car deal, and they know when a vehicle's price is "in the market" and "on the money." More and more, they don't like to negotiate deals the way their parents and grandparents did.

We discussed this shift in consumer expectations and the "rising tide of transparency" in Chapters 16 and 26. We noted how velocity dealers have shifted to a "documentation as negotiation" model where they consistently measure the discounts sales teams offer customers. At some stores, this exercise is not a key component of pay plans for sales associates.

The upshot: These dealers "hold gross" by offering competitive and market-transparent vehicle pricing and using real-time market data and documentation to justify price and minimize discounts. This is a nearly 180-degree shift for traditional sales teams. As noted in Chapter 22, this practice has velocity dealers "running to price" rather than running away from it as they increase sales, ROI and profitability in used vehicles.

9. **Dare to be different.** This road to reinvention commandment might be more bluntly expressed as "ditch tradition." But it's really more than that.

   I don't know any dealers who wouldn't agree that today's car business is more fast-changing than it's ever been. If you think about it, the past 10 years have rendered much of the traditional operating processes and principles irrelevant.

   In this challenging and exciting environment, reinvention-minded dealers must achieve a delicate balancing act: As they reinvent their dealership people and processes, they need to keep an eye on the future to ensure the changes they make today have relevance for tomorrow.

This is why I believe a "dare to be different" mindset is appropriate. Dealers must take calculated risks and test new ideas to keep ahead of the competition and stay on pace with the evolution of our business.

10. **Embrace performance improvement.** As dealers head down the road to reinvention, they will encounter setbacks and sometimes costly mistakes. This is, in fact, the nature of reinvention. It's a mix of trial, error and success.

The most successful reinvention-minded dealers recognize and embrace these reinvention realities. They invest the energy, resources and time to create a culture that strives for and rewards performance improvement.

They also view performance improvement more broadly than traditional dealers. It's not just about increased sales, ROI and profitability. It's about creating, managing and inspiring a team of players committed to doing their jobs better every day. These dealers lead by example, not merely the authority of their position.

This approach to leadership is effective and infectious, and it yields superior results, particularly with the incoming generation of salespeople and managers. I also recognize, however, that this leadership style often tests the drive and DNA of many dealers. We're all entrepreneurs, known for our out-size egos, risk-taking and larger-than-life personalities.

The key for reinvention success, in my view, rests with tempering these perfectly fine characteristics and rechanneling them in a manner that goes beyond the "get 'er done" mantra many of us bring to work every day.

The following quote from Mao Zedong is a helpful reminder of the leadership style dealers must adopt to achieve road to reinvention success: "Our attitude towards ourselves should be 'to be satiable in learning' and towards others 'to be tireless in teaching.'"[9]

---

9   http://thinkexist.com/quotation/our-attitude-towards-ourselves-should-be-to-be/533621.html

POSTSCRIPT: THE VELOCITY KOOL-AID ACID TEST

"Hey Dale...What happens if everyone drinks the velocity Kool-Aid?"

I hear this question on a near-daily basis. It most frequently comes from dealers who have embarked on the road to reinvention and begun to see gains in their used vehicle sales, return on investment (ROI) and profitability.

As they taste this renewed success, they start looking over their shoulders. They wonder what happens if every dealer adopts the Velocity Method of Management™ and sees similar results. They start to worry that the business will bottom out and no one will make any money.

Allow me to address this important question head-on: The "bottom out" scenario will never occur in used vehicles. Yes, it may become even more challenging and difficult to "win" in what will increasingly become a hyper-competitive, highly efficient and market-attuned retailing environment. But there will still be plenty of opportunity for dealers to profit and prosper.

I say this for three key reasons:

1. **Dealers are too diverse and diffuse as individuals.** Think of your last 20 Group meeting. I'd be willing to bet that, no matter the topic, each dealer had his/her own take on the discussion at hand. The same is true with the adoption of velocity principles and metrics.

   Simply put, some dealers do a better job of it than others. Some embrace the totality of the "wheel of fortune" in their dealerships, others believe each dealership department should operate on its own. Some aim to dominate their market, others seek a slightly bigger piece of the retailing pie. Some dealers will continue to rely on their new vehicle departments for the lion's share of their sales and profits, with used vehicles being an after-thought.

   The upshot: Even if velocity management becomes near-ubiquitous, there will never be a single, monolithic-style approach to managing used vehicle operations and making money in our business.

DALE POLLAK'S • vAuto

Kewl-Aid

All car dealers should drink twice daily for increased sales, faster velocity in turning inventory and greater financial success.

2. **Individual cars aren't "true" commodities.** While used vehicles are increasingly "commodity-like," individual cars are still unique. Each has its own strengths and weaknesses, both of which can vary depending on the interests and needs of a particular buyer. This means that it's unlikely two dealers would merchandise and sell the exact same car and do so in exactly the same manner, even if they both operated in the same market.

3. **The cycle of "efficient" markets.** I encourage dealers who fear the car business will "bottom

out" to consider the commodities markets. These are the long-established exchanges where investors and speculators bid for and buy grain, cattle, gold, oil and other commodities. These are widely regarded as the most "efficient" markets because buyers and sellers typically use the same information and resources as they make their respective decisions.

There is a fairly uniform dynamic to commodities markets that offers a glimpse of what life for dealers might be like *if* every dealer adopted velocity management principles and approached the used vehicle marketplace in a near-uniform manner.

In every market, there is a price at which any product or service will transact. The economists call this price the "equilibrium price" and traders call it the "margin price." So what would happen in the unlikely event that one day every dealer could see the margin price of their vehicles and was willing to move immediately to it? The effect would be that that margin price would undoubtedly move lower, producing a painful effect for all sellers.

Time-tested market experience assures us of what would happen next. Those sellers with the highest costs of operations (i.e. the least efficient sellers) will begin to systematically exit the market in favor of what they perceive to be better investment opportunities. For example, a soy bean trader with too many people on his or her payroll will conclude, when faced with a too-low margin price, that there are better opportunities in trading corn or some other more attractive commodity.

The used car manager standing in the lane, whose dealership charges vehicles with exorbitant costs and packs will likely conclude that they cannot make any money with fuel-efficient vehicles given the high cost of acquisition. This used car manager will also likely exit the fuel-efficient vehicle lane in favor of some other type of vehicle segment, like large SUVs, where they perceive a greater investment return. Similarly, automobile dealers who have failed to become more efficient will likely one day conclude that their dealership investment would yield a more attractive return if they exited the business, sold their real estate to the local developer and invested the remainder in high-yield bonds.

Once the least efficient sellers exit the market in favor of what they consider to be better investment opportunities, the margin price will begin to rise. Once the margin price begins to rise, the most efficient sellers who were able to ride out the cycle to the bottom will begin to enjoy significant profits due to their extraordinary operational efficiency. To be sure, once too many less-efficient sellers leave the market and the margin price rises high enough, it will once again attract less-efficient sellers and the process will repeat itself over and over again.

The lesson to be learned for automobile dealers from these markets is that there will certainly be ever greater price competition, what some might call a "race to the bottom". In fact, however, there will never be a situation where no one makes any money. Rather, the money will be made by those dealer/sellers that have embarked upon the road to reinvention and have made their dealerships the most efficient operations in their respective markets.

Index

CPSIA information can be obtained at www.ICGtesting.com
Printed in the USA
LVOW07*2155100316

478698LV00003B/3/P